T0318826

Preventing Child Maltreatment in the U.S.

Multicultural Considerations

Violence against Women and Children

Series editor, Judy L. Postmus

Millions of women and children are affected by violence across the globe. Gender-based violence affects individuals, families, communities, and policies. Our new series includes books written by experts from a wide range of disciplines including social work, sociology, health, criminal justice, education, history, and women's studies. A unique feature of the series is the collaboration between academics and community practitioners. The primary author of each book in most cases is a scholar, but at least one chapter is written by a practitioner, who draws out the practical implications of the academic research. Topics will include physical and sexual violence; psychological, emotional, and economic abuse; stalking; trafficking; and childhood maltreatment, and will incorporate a gendered, feminist, or womanist analysis. Books in the series are addressed to an audience of academics and students, as well as to practitioners and policymakers.

Hilary Botein and Andrea Hetling, *Home Safe Home: Housing Solutions for Survivors of Intimate Partner Violence*

Preventing Child Maltreatment miniseries:

Milton A. Fuentes, Rachel R. Singer, and Renee L. DeBoard-Lucas, *Preventing Child Maltreatment in the U.S.: Multicultural Considerations*

Esther J. Calzada, Monica Faulkner, Catherine A. LaBrenz, and Milton A. Fuentes, *Preventing Child Maltreatment in the U.S.: The Latinx Community Perspective*

Melissa Phillips, Shavonne Moore-Lobban, and Milton A. Fuentes, *Preventing Child Maltreatment in the U.S.: The Black Community Perspective*

Royleen J. Ross, Julii M. Green, and Milton A. Fuentes, *Preventing Child Maltreatment in the U.S.: American Indian and Alaska Native Perspectives*

Preventing Child Maltreatment in the U.S.

Multicultural Considerations

MILTON A. FUENTES, RACHEL R. SINGER, AND
RENEE L. DEBOARD-LUCAS

Rutgers University Press

New Brunswick, Camden, and Newark, New Jersey, and London

Library of Congress Cataloging-in-Publication Data

Names: Fuentes, Milton A., author. | Singer, Rachel R. (Psychologist), author. |
    Deboard-Lucas, Renee L., author.
Title: Preventing child maltreatment in the U.S. : multicultural considerations /
    Milton A. Fuentes, Rachel R. Singer, and Renee L. DeBoard-Lucas.
Description: New Brunswick, NJ : Rutgers University Press, [2022] | Series:
    Violence against women and children | Includes bibliographical references and
    index.
Identifiers: LCCN 2021055689 | ISBN 9781978822573 (paperback) |
    ISBN 9781978822580 (hardback) | ISBN 9781978822597 (epub) |
    ISBN 9781978822603 (mobi) | ISBN 9781978822610 (pdf)
Subjects: LCSH: Child abuse—United States. | Child abuse—United States—
    Prevention. | Child welfare—United States.
Classification: LCC HV6626.52 .F84 2022 | DDC 362.760973—dc23/
    eng/20220404
LC record available at https://lccn.loc.gov/2021055689

A British Cataloging-in-Publication record for this book is available from the
British Library.

References to internet websites (URLs) were accurate at the time of writing.
Neither the author nor Rutgers University Press is responsible for URLs that may
have expired or changed since the manuscript was prepared.

♾ The paper used in this publication meets the requirements of the American
National Standard for Information Sciences—Permanence of Paper for Printed
Library Materials, ANSI Z39.48-1992.

www.rutgersuniversitypress.org

Manufactured in the United States of America

Every moment is an organizing moment, every person a potential activist, every minute a chance to change the world.

—Dolores Huerta

Contents

Preventing Child Maltreatment in the U.S.

Multicultural Considerations

Introduction

It is easier to build strong children
than to repair broken adults.
—Frederick Douglass

Child maltreatment is a major public health concern, disproportionally affecting communities of color. This book is part of a concentrated
series of books that examines child maltreatment across minoritized,
cultural groups. Specifically, this volume examines core multicultural
concepts (e.g., intersectionality, acculturation, spirituality, oppression)
as they relate to child maltreatment in the United States, while the
other books take a closer look at particular ethnic or racial communities (e.g., Black, Latinx, American Indian and Alaska Native) in this
country. Additionally, this book examines child maltreatment through
the interaction of feminist, multicultural and prevention/wellness
promotion lenses. Recommendations for treatment in each book build
on a foundation of prevention and promotion, along with multicultural and feminist theories. The authors of this introductory volume
include an academician (Milton Fuentes) and two practitioners
(Rachel Singer and Renee DeBoard-Lucas); all of us are experts in
child maltreatment and multiculturalism. We take a culture-centered
approach, in which all aspects of child maltreatment are considered
through a cultural lens. Additionally, where relevant, we encourage readers to apply Goodman et al.'s (2004) six key social justice
principles, which are informed by feminist and multicultural theories.
These principles include engaging in self-examination; sharing power;

giving voice to the oppressed; raising consciousness; focusing on strengths and leaving clients with valuable tools. Lastly, throughout the book, five case studies, which are introduced in chapter 1, are revisited to help the readers make important and meaningful connections between theory and practice.

Engaging in Self-Examination and Understanding Positionality

As advised by numerous diversity experts (Falicov, [2013] 2014; Gallardo, 2014), it is critical for child maltreatment professionals to understand their own socio-cultural profiles and positions and how these factors may affect their work with clients, families and communities. This process, known as reflexivity (Cumming-Potvin, 2013), is associated with one of Goodman et al.'s (2004) principles, "engaging in self-examination," discussed further in chapter 4. To facilitate this process and model this best practice, what follow are the authors' self-reflective narratives. Practitioners are encouraged to consider our profiles as well as their own, as they work with their clients. More tools for facilitating this process are discussed in chapters 3 and 4.

Dr. Milton Fuentes is a light-skinned, Spanish-English bilingual Puerto Rican, who grew up in a "traditional" Puerto Rican household. His mother has a second-grade education and his father made it up to ninth grade; his parents both highly valued family, education and Catholicism. Hence, he attended private Catholic schools from first grade up to and including college. While he currently does not identify as Catholic, he does consider himself spiritual, meditating every day and embracing Buddhist ideology. While Fuentes's identity is quite nuanced, factors that inform his teaching, research, and practice include his light-skin privilege, his first-generation status, his bilingualism, and his ethnicity. When working with Latinx clients, Fuentes engages in a comparative process, recognizing the ways in which he is similar and dissimilar from them. While he prefers to use specific ethnic terms (e.g., Puerto Rican), at times he opts for the term Latinx to capture the diverse communities in the United States from Latin America and to be gender-inclusive. Dr. Fuentes strives to maintain humility, recognizing that the field of multiculturalism is dynamic and evolving; yet, that does not stop him from pursuing cultural excellence in his professional endeavors.

Dr. Rachel Singer identifies as White and Jewish (Sephardic and Ashkenazi). She is a third-generation immigrant whose grandfathers immigrated to the United States from Poland and the Ukraine, fleeing persecution due to their Jewish identities. Interwoven into her Jewish identity is the cultural principle of "Tikun Olam," which translates to a moral obligation to identify inequities in the world and aim to repair them. She recognizes that the intersecting aspects of her identity afford her both high and low power positions, depending on her interpersonal and social contexts. Dr. Singer's family and cultural histories have shaped her professional choices, including her current work conducting asylum evaluations of refugees. She works in an outpatient practice providing therapy with clients of all ages. Prior to working as a psychologist, Singer obtained her teaching certification in elementary education. She has taught elementary, college, and graduate level students.

Dr. Renee DeBoard-Lucas identifies as a White woman with a French and Pennsylvania Dutch background. She is a first-generation college graduate who recognizes and appreciates the opportunities that a college and graduate education has afforded her. This appreciation informs her supervision of mental health trainees, her clinical work with youth who have experienced abuse, neglect, or both, and her passion for advocacy. Over time, DeBoard-Lucas has become increasingly aware of the ways that her White privilege impacts her daily lived experience, and she attempts to use that privilege to amplify the voices of those whom her ancestors have oppressed. Dr. DeBoard-Lucas is committed to a lifelong journey of anti-racist work.

Feminist Theory

We examine child maltreatment through the lens of feminist theory. Feminist theory arose as an alternative to prevailing theories for understanding sexism, sexual exploitation, and women's psychological distress, oppression, and related inequality. A major aim of this approach is to analyze and dismantle the patriarchal system that leads to these pernicious dynamics (hooks, 2015). A key concept that emerged from this framework is intersectionality, which considers the "intersection" of various identities (e.g., gender, race, ethnicity, age) and its impact on one's identity and functioning, as it relates to power and privilege (Howard and Renfrow, 2014). Within feminist paradigms evolved other derivatives to more accurately portray and meet the needs of BIPOC communities (Black, Indigenous, and People of Color). For example, womanism centers the experiences, conditions, and concerns of Black women; it is a sociopolitical framework that centralizes gender concerns as well as other forms of oppression (race, class, sexuality) (Bryant-Davis and Comas-Diaz, 2016). Specifically, womanism "identifies and criticizes sexism in the Black American community and racism in the feminist community" (Longley, 2020, para. 2). Similarly, *mujerismo* expands traditional feminism "by focusing on the centrality of community, mutual caring, and global solidarity; while aiming towards collective liberation and transformation" (Bryant-Davis and Comas-Diaz, 2016, 10). Within Indigenous communities, traditional notions of feminism are rejected due to their ties to colonialism and oppression; instead, Indigenous feminism focuses on decolonization, promoting sovereignty and human rights, embracing the matriarch, and seeking wisdom from elders (Deer, 2019; Gearon, 2021). Ross et al. (forthcoming) use indigenous feminist principles to dismantle the deficit narrative proffered in the United States around Native communities and instead construct an accurate and strengths-based narrative that better serves their communities. For a deeper understanding of these various frameworks, we direct readers to other volumes in this series, which adopt and apply their respective feminist frameworks to their particular communities (Calzada et al., forthcoming; Phillips et al., forthcoming; Ross et al., forthcoming).

Borrowing from these various feminist tenets, throughout this book we consider how child maltreatment is caused and informed by patriarchal forces that promote the rights, privileges, power, and wellbeing of some over others in society. We pay special attention to women, children, and communities of color, and consider ways to enfranchise these populations. As we explore child maltreatment, we use these various feminist frameworks to understand key feminist concepts promoted by BIPOC scholars, such as intersectionality, critical consciousness, structural oppression, and empowerment.

Multicultural Theory

Over the past few decades, theoreticians and practitioners have started to appreciate the power and influence of culture on a person's wellbeing. For example, Pederson (1990) argued that the multicultural perspective had emerged as "fourth force" in mental health counselling arenas, following psychodynamic, behavioral, and humanistic frameworks. He observed that multiculturalism includes ethnographic variables (e.g., race, nationality, language), demographic variables (e.g., gender, age), and memberships, which are inclusive of the multiple contexts that individuals inhabit. These components reveal the complex and dynamic nature of multiculturalism. Also, recognizing the multidimensional, complex, and nuanced aspects of culture, (1983), a well-known multicultural scholar of Latinx and diverse communities offered the following definition of culture:

> Culture is those sets of shared world views, meanings, and adaptive
> behaviors derived from simultaneous membership and participation
> in a variety of contexts, such as language; rural, urban or suburban
> setting; race, ethnicity, and socioeconomic status; age, gender, gender
> identity, sexual orientation and sexual variance, religion, disability,
> nationality; employment, education and occupation, political
> ideology, stage of migration/acculturation, partaking of similar
> historical moments and ideologies (xiv–xv).

Most, if not all, helping professions require practitioners who address child maltreatment to understand the significant influence of culture and to develop wide-ranging competency in this key area. For example, the American Association for Marriage and Family Therapy (2015) not only aspires to embrace and maintain a diverse membership, but they are also committed to diversity and equity in all their endeavors including practice, research, and training. Additionally, the National Association of Social Workers (2013) requires child welfare practitioners to be responsive to a family's culture (e.g., values, customs, and beliefs), as they design their service plans. Finally, the American Psychological Association (APA) (2017b) urges psychologists who address child maltreatment to be cognizant of cultural differences, including factors such as age, gender, race, ethnicity, culture, disability, and socioeconomic status. The APA requires psychologists to eliminate or address any biases associated with these factors as they work with their clients. To guide these efforts, APA recently released the *Multicultural Guidelines: An Ecological Approach to Context, Identity, and Intersectionality* (APA, 2017b). These guidelines urge practitioners to engage in child maltreatment efforts that reduce trauma and promote resiliency in our communities, with a special focus on practice, research, and consultation. The guidelines are discussed extensively in chapters 3 and 4.

Social Justice: Where Feminism Meets Multiculturalism

Goodman et al. (2004) utilized tenets from both feminism and multiculturalism to identify six principles that practitioners can use in their efforts to promote social justice in child welfare and related social services. These principles include engaging in self-examination; sharing power; giving voice to the oppressed; raising consciousness; focusing on strengths; and leaving clients with valuable tools. Since then, other scholars have developed models that closely align with these principles. See, for example, French et al's (2020) Radical Healing Framework and the Healing Ethno and Racial Trauma (HEART) framework (Chavez-Dueñas et al., 2019); both of these models are discussed further in chapters 2, 3, and 4. Throughout this book, we apply these six principles in our efforts to better understand, prevent, and address child maltreatment. Chapter 4 provides an in-depth discussion of each principle and illustrates how they connect to our five cases.

Prevention and Wellness Promotion Theory

Finally, throughout this book, we also address child maltreatment through the public health framework promoted by the Centers for Disease Control and Prevention (CDC) (Anderson et al., 2019; CDC, n.d.-g), which attempts to prevent child maltreatment through a three-pronged approach: primary, secondary and tertiary. Hence, this framework considers the complexity of child maltreatment, as there are those children and families who can *potentially* be affected by child maltreatment, those who are *at-risk* of being affected by it, or those who *are* affected by it. Thus, the need for three types of prevention. This model is discussed further in chapter 3. In addition to prevention, community psychologists have long advocated for the promotion of wellness, arguing that that the absence of illness does not necessarily lead to optimal individual or community functioning (Jason et al., 2019). Instead, this branch of psychology asserts that wellness is a "combination of physical, psychological, and social health, including attainment of personal goals and well-being" (19). To this end, guided by Goodman et al.'s (2004) principles, in this book we enumerate numerous strategies for promoting wellness by focusing on strengths, raising consciousness, sharing power, empowering communities, and promoting advocacy.

Book Structure

Chapter 1 begins with an overview of child maltreatment. The chapter defines child maltreatment and identifies the various type of child maltreatment, including neglect, physical abuse, and sexual abuse, differentiating between acts of commission and acts of omission. Another section reviews the prevalence of child maltreatment. Chapter 1 also defines and discusses risk and protective factors associated with child maltreatment, providing an ecological framework to highlight its nuanced and complex nature. Specifically, the chapter looks at various elements that foster or prevent child maltreatment, including at individual, relational, community, and societal levels. Lastly, throughout this chapter and in each subsequent chapter relevant connections are made to the five case studies, exploring and applying the tenets of multiculturalism and feminism.

Chapter 2 introduces key multicultural theories and related core concepts as they relate to child maltreatment. Specifically, the chapter covers the systems approach, identity development theories, and ethnic-racial socialization theory, and explores key constructs that can inform the conceptualization of child maltreatment through a cultural lens, such as relational factors, acculturation, intersectionality, and power differentials. The main goal of chapter 2 is to provide a deep grounding of the theoretical tenets of multiculturalism.

Chapter 3 reviews major theoretical models related to wellness and prevention with a focus on primary, secondary and tertiary prevention levels. It gives considerable attention to protective factors and cultural strengths as they relate to child maltreatment. This chapter provides comprehensive coverage of evidence-based interventions for preventing and managing child maltreatment with a special emphasis on cultural factors and intersectionality. Chapter 3 concludes with a discussion of best practices associated with child maltreatment.

Chapter 4 explores the intersection of feminism and multiculturalism as it relates social justice and wellbeing by adopting Goodman et al.'s (2004) six key principles and considering their application to the management of child maltreatment. As noted earlier, these principles include engaging in self-examination; sharing power; giving voice to the oppressed; raising consciousness; focusing on strengths, and leaving clients with valuable tools. We offer a new framework for understanding and addressing child maltreatment with an emphasis on introspection, collaboration, strengths, and empowerment.

Finally, the book closes with chapter 5, which highlights major conclusions around child maltreatment, feminism, and multiculturalism. Final impressions and recommendations associated with the case studies are established. The book ends with helpful resources and provides recommended readings.

Closing Summary

This introduction showcases our reflexive narratives, provides overviews of the major theories that guide our work, and discusses the overall structure of the book. In the next chapter, we provide a thorough discussion of child maltreatment, introduce key terms, discuss the prevalence of child maltreatment across American society, and introduce the compelling case studies. We give special attention throughout the book to multicultural factors and how they inform child maltreatment.

1

Child Maltreatment

Each child belongs to all of us and
they will bring us a tomorrow in
direct relation to the responsibility
we have shown to them.
—Maya Angelou

This chapter highlights key issues related to child maltreatment, a major public health concern in the United States. According to the Administration on Children, Youth and Families (ACYF), an entity of the U.S. Department of Health and Human Services (HHS), there was a 3 percent increase in child maltreatment from 2012 to 2016, while 2015 to 2019 saw a 4 percent decrease in child maltreatment cases (U.S. Department of Health & Human Services, 2021). This trend represents a rate of approximately 8.9 victims per 1,000 children across the country. However, the COVID-19 pandemic will most likely reverse this downward trend. According to the World Health Organization (WHO, 2020), hotlines across the world are seeing an increase in maltreatment reports. They attribute this to stressed parents spending more time with their children; economic uncertainty; typical reporters, like teachers, having limited access to children; an increased use of alcohol and drugs; and child protective services not being able to properly assess and conduct routine home visits.

Moreover, child maltreatment can cause impairment in a child's neurological, psychological, social, and academic functioning (National Scientific Council on the Developing Child, 2020) and could result in death (U.S. Department of Health & Human Services, 2021). Additionally, the adverse childhood events associated with child maltreatment can lead to major problems in adulthood, including medical problems, smoking, suicidality, or early adult death (Felitti et al., 2019). The present chapter defines child maltreatment, discusses its prevalence in American society, considers the major risk and protective factors associated with it, and begins to explore relevant connections among child maltreatment, race, and ethnicity. It also reviews five case studies that illustrate potential instances of child maltreatment. Chapter 1 focuses more on the essential defining child maltreatment features in the cases, while the subsequent chapters consider the multicultural and feminist aspects as well as the related child maltreatment implications for prevention and intervention.

The Case of Jaquann. Jaquann was a fifteen-year-old, African American youth, who lived with his mother and younger siblings in an urban city. The family had a number of financial difficulties, and Jaquann's mother had recently returned to work after a period of unemployment. Shortly after she began her new job, Jaquann was robbed at gunpoint on his way to the school bus. He developed posttraumatic stress symptoms following this event, which also triggered memories and symptoms related to previous violent events he had experienced and witnessed. Jaquann wanted to go to school but was afraid of encountering the people who robbed him again if he went to the bus stop. He also knew that he would not be able to concentrate in class because he kept experiencing intrusive images and thoughts related to these events. Jaquann stopped going to school. He did not tell his mother this, nor that he was robbed, as he did not like talking about his feelings and did not want to worry her more. He had missed several weeks of school before his mother got a notice that she was being reported for child neglect due to his prolonged absences. When Jaquann called his guidance counselor to find out how he could make up some of the missed work or if he could enroll in home schooling, she said, "Oh, I'm surprised to hear from you; I thought you had dropped out."

What Is Child Maltreatment?

The case of Jaquann and others introduced later in this chapter typify various forms of child maltreatment. Child maltreatment is defined as "any recent act or failure to act on the part of a parent or caretaker which results in death, serious physical or emotional harm, sexual abuse or exploitation; or an act or failure to act, which presents an imminent risk of serious harm" (U.S. Department of Health & Human Services, 2021, 16). Major types of child maltreatment include neglect, physical abuse, psychological maltreatment, and sexual abuse. These types are also categorized as acts of omission or acts of commission (Child Welfare Information Gateway, 2018). As the terms suggest, acts of **commission** involve engaging in direct actions that are detrimental to a child's welfare (i.e., all forms of abuse), while acts of **omission** involve failing to perform certain responsibilities that are critical to a child's welfare (i.e., all forms of neglect) (Child Welfare Information Gateway, 2018).

Neglect

Neglect refers to the failure of a caregiver to provide necessary and developmentally appropriate care, despite having the financial means to provide the care (U.S. Department of Health & Human Services, 2021). There are various types of neglect, including physical neglect, emotional neglect, medical neglect, educational neglect, and inadequate supervision. All of these types are considered acts of omission. The following case of Bashiir highlights the challenges faced by an immigrant family in the United States that led to particular circumstances that may suggest neglect. While a cursory review might suggest clear maltreatment, a deeper analysis is needed to fully appreciate the complex and nuanced aspects of this narrative.

The Case of Bashiir. Bashiir was a 16-year-old Black male from Somalia. He and his parents immigrated to the United States with his six siblings. Prior to arriving in the United States, Bashiir and his family spent two years living in refugee camps. Bashiir was responsible for taking care of his six younger siblings while the parents were at work. Both parents worked multiple jobs. Bashiir was referred for therapy by his school due to frequent absences. They reported concerns about potential neglect, as the parents were not able to be present at home during daytime hours or after school to take care of the children. Bashiir expressed in therapy that he wanted to get an education, but he felt responsible for his siblings. He indicated that his parents had frequently reminded him that his first obligation was to his family, and that school was secondary. Bashiir also noted that he was worried about the safety of his younger siblings (ages 1, 3, 4, 7, 11, and 14) on the days when he did go to school, as they were by themselves and there was frequent gang activity and community violence in the neighborhood. When the therapist asked the parents to come to treatment, Bashiir's mother first asked that the community elders come to a session to find out the therapist's intentions. Both parents indicated that they were not available for therapy sessions due to their rigorous work schedules.

Case Discussion. The case of Bashiir and Jaquann (discussed earlier) illustrate different forms of potential neglect. Again, neglect is an act of omission and suggests that the caregivers are not providing necessary and developmentally appropriate care. In Bashiir's case, his parents were not ensuring that Bashiir was attending school on a regular basis, while with Jaquann, his mother did not know that he was not attending school. These omissions could be considered educational neglect. While educational requirements vary across states in the United States, generally parents are required to enroll their children in an academic program by age six and keep them enrolled until they are at least sixteen years of age; make sure they attend school consistently; and ensure any special needs are addressed by their children's schools (National Center for Education Statistics, 2017). Later in this book, we will analyze these cases through alternative lenses and consider related core multicultural concepts, cultural strengths, and feminist implications. For example, a cursory discussion of the cases of Bashiir and Jaquann fail to consider systemic forces that may inform the family's circumstances as well as familial or cultural strengths they may possess. For instance, in the case of Bashiir, culture of origin factors may be informing this case (e.g., school attendance expectations and practices in Somalia), while identity factors, such as ethnicity, race, age, class, and gender, inform both the cases of Bashiir and Jaquann.

Physical Abuse
Physical abuse, an act of commission, involves physical acts that cause or have the potential to cause physical harm to a child (U.S.

Department of Health & Human Services, 2021). Examples include hitting, kicking, shaking, biting, and other physical acts that can cause injury. On the surface, the following case of Amelia could be considered an example of physical abuse. However, when examined more closely, the reader will note the challenges faced by a Latinx family that values raising well-behaved, obedient and respectful children—all values that are aligned with the parents' cultural worldviews.

The Case of Amelia. Amelia was a fourteen-year-old Latina youth whose family fled to the United States from Venezuela when she was ten years old to escape political unrest and persecution. Amelia was fluent in English and her parents were not, so they relied on her to serve as their translator. Lately, Amelia had been coming home from school and talking back to her parents about household chores she was supposed to complete. She used the phrase "F-this" frequently, used an aggressive tone, and rolled her eyes. One morning, her parents asked her to take out the garbage and Amelia responded, "F-this" and pushed a chair out of her way to take the garbage out. Her parents did not appreciate her tone and her mother responded with a *tapa boca* (cover the mouth). *Tapa boca* is a physical punishment where the back of the hand, open handed, is used to slap the mouth of another. However, Amelia immediately began to bleed due to her braces and went to school with a bloody mouth. When asked by her teacher what had happened, Amelia rolled her eyes and stated that her mother hit her. Amelia's teacher immediately called the Department of Children and Families.

Case Discussion. The case of Amelia may suggest several forms of child maltreatment. The most obvious type may be physical abuse. Physical abuse includes acts that can cause physical harm to a child. In this case, the mother's attempt to discipline Amelia resulted in a physical injury. One could argue that the mother lacked the necessary knowledge and skills to adequately discipline Amelia, leading to other potential forms of child maltreatment, such as inadequate supervision or emotional neglect. Furthermore, not much is known about the mother's discipline philosophy and related values. In the chapters that follow, we will explore the systemic and feminist forces that inform this account and how cultural values and family strengths could be leveraged to properly support Amelia and her family.

Sexual Abuse

Sexual abuse, another type of child maltreatment, involves engaging a child in sexual activity for sexual gratification or financial benefit to the perpetrator. Sexual abuse includes "contacts for sexual purposes, molestation, statutory rape, prostitution, pornography, exposure, incest, or other sexually exploitative activities" (U.S. Department of Health & Human Services, 2021, 128). Sexual abuse falls into the acts of commission category.

The Case of Miguelina. Miguelina Sanchez, a fourteen-year-old girl of Mexican descent, was referred to the local family placement and prevention program in New York city by the child protective bureau office due to a substantiated a case of sexual abuse. During the initial assessment, the treating psychologist, Dr. Ortiz, learned that Miguelina was being sexual abused by her brother, Tomas Sanchez (age twenty-two). The abuse occurred for over eight years and included fondling, digital penetration, and oral sex. When Miguelina's parents discovered that Tomas was going to be prosecuted and could face jail time, they quickly sent him to Mexico to live with extended family members. As Dr. Ortiz conducted the assessment and initial treatment, it was clear that sexual abuse had occurred; however, Miguelina did not see it that way, claiming that it was a shared romance between her and her brother. As was the case with many families Dr. Ortiz had worked with, during the course of treatment other forms of child maltreatment were revealed, including intimate partner violence between Mr. and Mrs. Sanchez and emotional abuse toward Miguelina by Mr. Sanchez. In sessions, Miguelina reported witnessing the intimate partner violence and not being sure why her mother did not stop it. At times she felt scared in her home and feared for her mother's safety. Miguelina also recounted how her father often used derogatory terms with the women in the family, reporting that he often called her stupid and stated that she would never amount to anything.

Case Discussion. The case of Miguelina meets the criteria for sexual abuse, as it involves an older person engaging in sexual acts for sexual gratification. However, beyond the technical nuances of the sexual abuse, there are larges forces at play that warrant further exploration. Sexual abuse does not occur in a vacuum; it occurs in complex and dynamic contexts. Considering the models introduced in the previous chapter as well as the ecological model discussed later in this chapter (see "Protective Factors") and throughout this book, we need to understand and address the social determinants that permit the sexual exploitation of children, especially girls. We also need to comprehend the role the family's ethnicity plays in their narrative. Additionally, this case also illustrates how physical and sexual abuse can occur with psychological maltreatment, which will be discussed in the next section.

Psychological Maltreatment

Lastly, psychological or emotional maltreatment can involve acts of commission or omission, not involving physical abuse or sexual abuse. These acts can place children at risk for or are responsible for causing affective, cognitive, conduct, or other behavioral disorders. As noted by DePanfilis (2006), this type of maltreatment is difficult to assess and corroborate, but its effects on a child can be substantial and long lasting. Psychological maltreatment frequently involves verbal abuse or excessive demands on a child's performance (U.S. Department of Health & Human Services, 2021). Several studies have found that the co-occurrence of psychological maltreatment and other types of abuse or neglect was associated with more problematic outcomes (Spinazzola et al., 2014; Trickett et al., 2011). This was evident in the case of Miguelina, where her father engaged in verbal abuse (i.e., act of commission), calling her stupid and questioning her worth, while denying her the warmth and support needed by a child from their caregivers (i.e., act of omission). Later in the book we examine how patriarchal forces contribute to these deleterious dynamics and explore how adopting feminist and multicultural principles might help prevent and/or address them.

Prevalence of Child Maltreatment

In 1988, the Child Abuse and Prevention Act (CAPTA) was amended, requiring the Secretary of HHS to collect data on child maltreatment from all fifty states, the District of Columbia, and Puerto Rico. This amendment led to the establishment of the National Child Abuse and Neglect Data System, allowing ACYF to provide annual reports on child maltreatment. In their most current report released in 2021, which marked the thirtieth year edition of the Child Maltreatment report series, the most common types of abuse in 2019 were neglect (74.9%), physical abuse (17.5%), and sexual abuse (9.3%). A closer look at child victim demographics revealed that the youngest children were the most at risk for child maltreatment. Specifically, nearly 25.7 percent of all child victims were below the age of one, followed by almost 32 percent of victims between the ages of one and three (U.S. Department of Health & Human Services, 2021).

With respect to race and ethnicity, the ACYF 2019 victim statistics revealed some interesting trends. When looking at the rates per 1,000 children across all types of child maltreatment, the American Indian or Alaska Native group had the highest rate at 14.8 percent and the Black group followed with 13.8 percent. While the Asian group was the lowest at 1.7 percent, the Pacific Islander rate was 10.7 percent. The Hispanic rate per 1,000 children was 8.1 percent, while the White rate was 7.8 percent. Interestingly, the multiple race rate per 1,000 children was 11 percent. These figures clearly reveal that race and ethnicity are important variables to consider when understanding, managing and preventing child maltreatment as well as related disparities.

Regarding the perpetrators of child maltreatment, there were several notable observations. First, perpetrators were the individuals who committed or knowingly allowed the abuse and neglect to occur (U.S. Department of Health & Human Services, 2021). Second, the majority of the perpetrators were between the ages of eighteen and forty-four (83.1%) and women (53%), when combining all types of child maltreatment (U.S. Department of Health & Human Services, 2021). However, gender varies based on the type of maltreatment. For example, most sexual abuse instances are perpetrated by men (National Sexual Violence Resource Center, 2015). Third, the three largest groups of perpetrators were either White (48.9%), Black (21%), or Hispanic (19.7%) (U.S. Department of Health & Human Services, 2021). Lastly, in the majority of the cases (77.5%), the perpetrators were the caregivers (i.e., parents) of the child victims (U.S. Department of Health & Human Services, 2021).

Another important and relevant characteristic associated with child maltreatment trends is the racial and ethnic disproportionality (i.e., overrepresentation) and disparity (i.e., unequal outcomes) in the child welfare system. A brief issued by the Child Welfare Information Gateway (2016), an entity of the Children's Bureau, provides an interesting review of the literature in this area. The brief observed that Black or African American and Native American families were overrepresented in the child welfare system, while Asian and Hispanic families were underrepresented. The brief provided four possible explanations for these outcomes, including "disproportionate and disparate needs of children and families of color, particularly due to higher rates of poverty; racial bias and discrimination exhibited by individuals (e.g., caseworkers, mandated and other reporters); child welfare system factors (e.g., lack of resources for families of color, caseworker characteristics); and geographic context, such as the region, state, or neighborhood" (5). The authors concluded that cultural competence and bias management were key to addressing these concerning trends. Notably, Harris and Hacket (2008) found that professionals, who perceive the court system to be fair and rational, were unlikely to monitor proceedings for racial biases and unlikely to pursue training to enhance their cultural competency or increase their cultural consciousness. Additionally, in medical settings, Hymel et al. (2018) found that physicians were two times more likely to suspect and report abusive head trauma in racial/ethnic minority children. Chapters 3 and 4 will identify and discuss key strategies for addressing racial disproportionality and disparities in the child welfare system with an emphasis on the multicultural concepts outlined in chapter 2.

Sex Trafficking

Notably, in 2018, ACYF (U.S. Department of Health & Human Services, 2021) added sex trafficking to their types of child maltreatment, allowing states to report on its occurrence. Sex trafficking involves "recruitment, harboring, transportation, provision, or obtaining of a person for the purpose of a commercial sex act" (96). In order to better understand this new category, states are being advised to report sex trafficking separately and not in conjunction with sexual abuse (U.S. Department of Health & Human Services, 2021).

In 2019, 877 unique cases were identified by twenty-nine states with the overwhelming majority of victims being female (88.5%) and between the ages of fifteen and seventeen (63%). The U.S. Department of Justice (2011) also observed an overrepresentation of youth and racial/ethnic minorities. Specifically, when examining victim characteristics in 526 cases of human trafficking (e.g., sex trafficking and labor trafficking) between 2008 and 2010, 49 percent of the cases were age seventeen or younger; 32 percent were Black/African American, 25 percent were Latinx, and 20 percent were White. Lastly, Fedina et al. (2016) examined risk factors associated with child sex trafficking in the United States. In addition to also noting an overrepresentation of racial/ethnic minority victims, they also found that youth who had a history of running away from home, rape, and sexual abuse, were at higher risk for commercial sexual exploitation. These scholars recommended developing more comprehensive anti-trafficking legislation that could inform sound collaborative and inter-agency models for managing child sex trafficking as well as developing intervention programs that prevent or address the related risk factors.

Factors Related to Child Maltreatment

Risk Factors

Risk factors are characteristics associated with a child or caregiver that can lead to or increase the chances of child maltreatment (U.S. Department of Health & Human Services, 2021). The Centers for Disease Control and Prevention (CDC, n.d.-a) classifies these risk factors into four major categories: individual, relational, community, and societal factors. Within the individual category, they observed that children under the age of four and those with special needs are at greatest risk for child maltreatment. Within the relational category, certain background characteristics of perpetrators increase the child maltreatment risk. For example, caregivers with a history of child abuse or neglect or who lack basic child knowledge (e.g., typical developmental behaviors), are more likely to perpetrate child maltreatment. Additionally, as noted earlier, ACYF (U.S. Department of Health & Human Services, 2021) found that over 83.1 percent of the perpetrators who engaged in child maltreatment occurrences were between the ages of eighteen and forty-four. Moreover, the CDC (n.d.-a) noted that social isolation, intimate partner violence, and parenting stress could all contribute toward child maltreatment. Within the community category, community violence and factors related to neighborhood resources, such as poverty, high unemployment rates, and residential instability, are all associated with child maltreatment. Finally, the societal category includes social norms, laws, and policies that may contribute toward child maltreatment. Factors within this category can include favorable attitudes toward corporal punishment and laws that allow physical discipline.

The CDC (n.d.-a) recognizes that while children are not responsible for the maltreatment they experience, the presence of individual and other factors heighten the risk for child maltreatment. They also emphasize that these factors are associated with child maltreatment and may or may not be the exact causes of it. For example, children with developmental disabilities may be less able to understand that what happened to them was wrong and may be less likely to disclose abuse compared to their typically developing peers.

Given the relevance of these risk factors with child maltreatment, the National Child Abuse and Neglect Data System routinely assesses for nine child risk factors and twelve caregiver risk factors. In 2016, the ACYF focused on four major caregiver risk factors including alcohol abuse, drug abuse, financial problems, and inadequate housing, while in 2021, they highlighted several other risk factors including domestic violence, public assistance involvement, and any disability affecting a caregiver.

Physical Punishment. Physical punishment, which is typically administered by caregivers, is one important and well-known risk factor that is linked to the relational category. Physical punishment, also known as corporal punishment (e.g., "spanking") is defined as "non-injurious, openhanded hitting with the intention of modifying child behavior" (Gershoff & Grogan-Kaylor, 2016, 453). Gershoff and Gorgan-Kaylor (2016) conducted a meta-analysis of seventy-five studies focusing on spanking, which they defined as striking a child with an open hand on the buttocks or other extremities. These scholars concluded that there was a significant correlation between parental spanking and unfavorable child outcomes. Specifically, they noted that parental spanking was associated with more child-based aggression, more mental health problems, such as internalizing and externalizing problems, and more problematic parent-child relationships. Additionally, spanking was associated with lower self-esteem, poorer cognitive abilities, and inferior moral internalization (i.e., learning and adopting socially acceptable behaviors). These outcomes are especially concerning, given that spanking is the most common form of physical punishment in the United States.

Gershoff (2013) also discussed how culture, namely race and ethnicity, informed problematic outcomes associated with physical punishment. Specifically, she considered the cultural normativeness hypothesis (Lansford et al., 2005), which conjectured that children from cultural groups where physical punishment was a norm were less likely to experience problematic outcomes. In her review of the literature, she concluded that "in studies using longitudinal and nationally representative data, spanking predicted increases in children's problem behavior over time across White, Black, Latino, and Asian subsamples" (Gershoff, 2013, 135), debunking the cultural normativeness hypothesis.

Relatedly, researchers examined the relationship between child maltreatment and delinquency in 2,335 African American adolescent males (Williams et al., 2010). Their multivariate logistic regression models revealed that those participants who had experienced child maltreatment (i.e., neglect, physical abuse, sexual abuse, or a combination) were more likely to have a juvenile delinquency petition than those who had not experienced child maltreatment. This likelihood increased if there were multiple maltreatment reports, mental health treatment history, victimization, and a parent who had not completed high school.

Gershoff and Grogan-Kaylor's (2016) meta-analysis revealed that the more children were spanked the greater the chances that they would be physically abused. Interestingly, they emphasized that "spanking and physical abuse may have similar associations with child outcomes. . . . The association only indicates that milder and more severe corporal punishment are linked, and that the former may increase the risk that children will also be physically abused" (464). Confirming these assertions through experimental designs is not possible due to ethical concerns, as children cannot be assigned to "hit" and "no hit" experimental conditions. However, it is possible to examine the overall science associated with physical punishment and make a causal inference. To this end, Gershoff et al. (2018) reviewed the empirical research on child maltreatment and physical punishment and found that it met the criteria to make causal conclusions, noting that regardless of cultural, family, and neighborhood contexts, children who experienced physical punishment could experience the same harms that were associated with physical abuse. Given the detrimental outcomes associated with physical punishment, these scholars instructed parents not to use it and encouraged psychologists to discourage its practice. Additionally, they urged policy makers to educate the public on the hazards associated with physical punishment and promulgate more effective and optimal alternatives. However, despite these cautionary recommendations, physical punishment is still used and respected in many communities (Gershoff & Grogan-Kaylor, 2016). For example, a 2012 national survey found that over 94 percent of parents reported spanking their children and the majority felt that at times children needed a "good hard spanking" (Child Trends, 2013). The survey also revealed that Black and Hispanic mothers were more likely to endorse this sentiment. In the chapters that follow, we will discuss this literature further and consider the myriad of factors that inform this practice, considering the relevant familial, cultural, and feminist nuances.

Banning Physical Punishment. Several prominent organizations have taken a firm position against the physical discipline of children by parents, including the American Academy of Pediatrics, the American Medical Association, and the U.S. Centers for Disease Control and Prevention (APA, 2019). In 2019, the APA joined these organizations, noting that "scientific evidence demonstrates the negative effects of physical discipline of children by caregivers and thereby recommends that caregivers use alternative forms of discipline that are associated with more positive outcomes for children" (2).

Across the world, there are also efforts to end the physical punishment of children. For example, the Global Partnership to End Violence Against Children (2022) engages in efforts to reform laws across the world to prohibit and eliminate the corporal punishment of children. They argue that the sanctioning of corporal punishment by countries violates the rights of children because it prevents equal protection under the law, as interpersonal violence toward adults is typically illegal. To date sixty-three countries have banned the use of corporal punishment with children, while twenty-six other countries have expressed a commitment to reforming their laws to abolish it (Global Partnership to End Violence Against Children, 2018).

Transgender and Gender Nonbinary Children. Transgender and gender-nonbinary youth are at higher risk for child maltreatment and are more likely to experience various forms of oppression, such as cisgenderism and transmisogyny. An earlier study found that out of 109 study participants with gender dysphoria more than 25 percent reported experiencing child maltreatment (Bandini et al., 2011). Moreover, those who had experienced child maltreatment also revealed a worse lifetime mental health trajectory and higher body dissatisfaction.

Later, Thoma et al. (2021) surveyed 1,856 adolescents within a national sample and found that transgender adolescents, compared to their cisgender counterparts, were more likely to report various types of child maltreatment. Specifically, the maltreatment types included psychological abuse (73%), physical abuse (39%), and sexual abuse (19%). Additionally, transgender adolescents assigned female at birth had the highest risk for psychological abuse.

While transgender and gender-nonbinary children need specialized support, APA (2021b) cautions against gender identity change efforts, as they are associated with numerous problematic outcomes, including stigma, discrimination, and psychological distress. Instead, APA recommends engaging in gender affirming practices, as they have been found to promote self-determination, foster quality of life and psychological functioning, improve clinical treatment involvement, and decrease psychological distress. APA offers numerous resources to best serve this community and they can be found in the resources section of chapter 5.

Protective Factors

Protective factors associated with child maltreatment include elements that are found in families or communities that may lessen or prevent the likelihood of abuse or neglect from occurring (CDC, n.d.-a). Most protective factors are based in the familial context and include resources such as adequate housing, access to healthcare services, and funds to address concrete needs (e.g., food, clothing). Other protective factors are relational in nature and include parents or caregivers that are stable and can provide ongoing nurturance and supervision.

Since families do not exist in a vacuum, the larger context plays a significant role in ensuring an optimal environment free of child maltreatment. Bronfenbrenner (1977), a well-known developmental theorist, developed an ecological systems theory for understanding the complexity of human development. Within this framework, various systems (i.e., micro, meso, exo, and macro) each exert a unique influence. For example, in the micro system, that is, settings that have direct contact with the child (e.g., home, school), there may be well-equipped parents or teachers who have the necessary knowledge, skills, and attitudes to prevent the occurrence of child maltreatment. Additionally, in the exo system, that is, settings that affect, but do not have direct contact with the child (e.g., parent's place of employment, school board), there may be resources in place that promote optimal parenting. For example, a parent's place of employment may offer parenting classes or have family-friendly policies, allowing for positive youth development. As noted by the CDC (n.d.-b), communities that support families, take a strong position against child maltreatment, and promote child growth and resilience can serve as a protective factor. Essentially, families in resource-rich communities, who have access to gainful employment, strong support networks, and positive role models or mentors are less likely to engage in child maltreatment. The next chapter will examine these systems further.

Regretfully, protective factors have not been studied as extensively as risk factors and thus merit additional attention (CDC, n.d.-b). Chapter 3 takes a closer look at the current research on protective factors. Specifically, the chapter considers how strength-based approaches coupled with prevention programs that are culturally aligned can ensure the presence of protective factors and facilitate conditions that are optimal for childhood wellbeing.

Impact of Child Maltreatment

Child maltreatment has both short-term and long-term effects on its victims. The National Scientific Council on the Developing Child (2020) acknowledges the short-term effects of child maltreatment, noting that child maltreatment hinders development and causes psychological harm. While the response to trauma will vary depending on child's age, maturity, cultural background, access to resources, and other factors, immediate distress is usually a universal response (National Scientific Council on the Developing Child, 2020). Without the proper intervention, untreated trauma may cause impaired functioning at home and school as well as with peers. Specifically, the maltreated child may experience impaired sleep, fears, sadness, anger, irritability, separation anxiety, concentration concerns, and problems with schoolwork (APA, 2008). Neurological research in this area has grown considerably, acknowledging that childhood trauma affects brain development. Specifically, child maltreatment can prevent the proper development of the amygdala and the hippocampus, affect the regulation of cortisol hormone levels, and inhibit the proper functioning of the corpus callosum (National Scientific Council on the Developing Child, 2020; Silva, 2011). These are all critical systems that when compromised can affect behavioral and emotional functioning by thwarting focused attention, impulse control, and more advanced cognitive skills (National Scientific Council on the Developing Child, 2020).

Child maltreatment is also associated with concerning long-term effects. Widom (2014) introduces a schematic model that considers the cascade of long-term consequences that may occur after child abuse and neglect. In this model, the author highlights the interrelationships between the child, family, and community, recognizing that these various systems overlap, influencing each other and the child. Within this model, she categorizes the long-term consequences of child maltreatment into the following four domains: cognitive/intellectual, social/behavioral, psychological/emotional, and medical/physical. Some problematic adult outcomes associated with child maltreatment include increased risk for academic problems, revictimization, substance abuse, diabetes, and lung disease (Widom, 2014). For an in-depth discussion of this area, the reader is directed to Widom's (2014) review in the *Handbook of Child Maltreatment*.

In their frequently cited study, Felitti et al. (1998) were among the first investigators to systematically examine the impact of child maltreatment on adults. The researchers surveyed 9,508 adults who had completed a medical questionnaire in a large health maintenance organization about adverse childhood events, also known as ACES. The ACES included seven categories, comprising "psychological, physical, or sexual abuse; violence against mother; or living with household members who were substance abusers, mentally ill or suicidal, or ever imprisoned" (245). The study then examined the relationship between these ACES and other health outcomes, such as adult risk behavior, health status, and disease.

The researchers found that more than half of the respondents had experienced at least one adverse childhood event, while a quarter had experienced two or more events. They also identified a graded relationship between the identified ACES and diseases and risk behaviors in adulthood. Specifically, as the number of ACES increased so did the risk for alcoholism, smoking, depression, suicide attempts and other problematic behaviors. Similarly, the presence of ACES increased the likelihood for diseases in adulthood, such as cancer, liver disease, chronic lung disease, skeletal fractures, and ischemic heart disease. These findings have been corroborated over the years, including in a 2019 study (Felitti et al., 2019). While the authors recognized that the categories under study were interrelated, they concluded that individuals with multiple adverse childhood events were likely to have numerous health risk concerns later in life.

Child Fatalities

Child fatalities are another tragic outcome of child maltreatment. Krugman and Lane (2014) note that the major causes of child fatalities include abusive head trauma, Munchausen's Syndrome by Proxy, suffocation by SIDS, lethal poisoning, and fatal neglect. Between 2012 and 2016, the number of fatalities associated with abuse and neglect increased from 1,551 in 2013 to 1,700 in 2016 (U.S. Department of Health & Human Services, 2018), while 2019 saw 1,840 fatalities (U.S. Department of Health & Human Services, 2021). The states with the highest fatalities in 2019 were Texas (219), California, (149) and Indiana (116). The overwhelming majority (79.7%) of these fatalities were caused by biologically related caregivers (U.S. Department of Health & Human Services, 2021).

Interestingly, the 2019 fatalities shared some common characteristics. For example, most children were boys, many under the age of three. Additionally, when comparing this data with population data (per 100,000), racial disparities emerged. African American children were two times more likely than White children and three times more likely than Latinx children to experience a child maltreatment fatality (U.S. Department of Health & Human Services, 2021). Pacific Islander children followed Black children with a rate of 3.34 per 100,00 children and multiracial children had a rate of 3.07 per 100,000 children (U.S. Department of Health & Human Services, 2021).

Given this devastating outcome, understanding child maltreatment and considering ways to prevent it are essential to preventing these fatalities. Krugman and Lane (2014) observed that two key strategies to prevent child maltreatment fatalities include parent education and home visitation, but argue that widespread implementation could be costly and prohibitive. They conclude, though, that "increased provision of effective strategies such as education in the newborn period, new parent support via home visitation, and community involvement in assuring healthy families will be the only way to significantly reduce the rates of fatal child abuse" (109).

However, another way to prevent child fatalities is to understand the determinants that undergird abuse and neglect. This critical approach allows for a deeper analysis, attempting to understand the insidious effects of oppression towards women, children, and communities of color and how they inform child fatalities and child maltreatment. The next section pursues this view by adopting a feminist lens.

Feminist Theory and Child Maltreatment

As noted in the introduction, feminist theory is a framework that examines the role of a patriarchal social system in creating, maintaining, and fostering sexism, sexual exploitation, and oppression (hooks, 2015). Numerous scholars have examined the intersection of feminist theory and child maltreatment (Featherstone & Fawcett, 1994; Lancaster & Lumb, 1999; Namy et al., 2017), noting for example, that childhood sexual abuse of girls can be attributed to the ills of a patriarchal social system. The research has clearly established that girls are more than five times more likely to experience sexual abuse in their lifetime than boys (Finkelhor et al., 2014), and in the overwhelming majority of the cases the perpetrators are men (National Sexual Violence Resource Center, 2015). These findings clearly implicate a patriarchal infrastructure that promotes and maintains the sexual exploitation of girls and sanctions these unacceptable patterns.

Additionally, as noted earlier, women were slightly more likely than men to be identified as perpetrators of child maltreatment (54%). However, when considered through a feminist lens, Phillimore (n.d.) argued that these "mothers are more likely to be in a situation where they will be poor and under stress." Specifically, the National Women's Law Center (n.d.) asserted, "too many single mothers live in poverty. Women are overrepresented in low-wage jobs despite better educational credentials than ever. And unemployment rates remain painfully high for some groups of women" (para. 1). Additionally, research has found that the context for other forms of child abuse involves intimate partner violence, which is mostly perpetrated by men. Nonetheless, Child Protective Services often blames the mothers, withholds vital resources from the families, and threatens to remove the children (Fentiman, 2017; Stark & Flitcraft, 1988). Some scholars asserted that:

> The combination of male control, misleading psychological knowledge about women's propensity for "bonding," and sanctions used to enforce gender stereotypes of motherhood combine to increase the entrapment and inequality from which battering and child abuse originate [. . . .] The best way to prevent child abuse is through female empowerment (Stark & Flitcraft, 1988, 97).

Given that neglect, in all of its identified forms, is the largest type of child maltreatment (U.S. Department of Health & Human Services, 2021), these above-referenced factors and trends are very relevant, as they clearly point to the deleterious consequences of the established patriarchal social system that continues to absolve men and condemn women, contributing to child maltreatment.

Moreover, with respect to child maltreatment, one could argue that the pernicious tenets of the patriarchal social system that disadvantages women operates similarly for children. Milne (2013) authored a comprehensive discussion on the history of children in the world, describing a troubling past, in which children were ill-treated, victimized, considered property, and denied essential human rights. These historical accounts are corroborated by deMause (2002), a psychohistorian, who in his book, *The Emotional Life of Nations*, provides a grueling historical depiction of the evolution of child rearing, including disheartening narratives of abandonment, mutilation, physical and sexual abuse, and even death through child sacrifices. Childhood at that time was depicted as so horrific that St. Augustine was quoted as saying "Who would not shudder if he were given the choice of eternal death or life again as a child? Who would not choose to die?" (DeMause, 2002.)

Furthermore, more recently, UNICEF (n.d.-c) noted that:

> In the industrialized countries of the early twentieth century, there were no standards of protection for children. It was common for them to work alongside adults in unsanitary and unsafe conditions. Growing recognition of the injustices of their situation, propelled by greater understanding of the developmental needs of children, led to a movement to better protect them. International standards on child

rights have advanced dramatically over the past century, but gaps
remain in meeting those ideals (para 1–2).

The first formal effort to advance the rights of children globally was
in 1924 when the League of Nations adopted the Geneva Declaration
on the Rights of a Child. This declaration recognized children as a special class that required support, protection, and societies that promoted their wellbeing (UNICEF, n.d.- c). Over the past thirty years,
considerable efforts have been made to protect children, recognize
them as human beings, and advance their rights. Specifically, in 1989,
the United Nations introduced to the General Assembly the Convention on the Rights of the Child, an international treaty that recognized children as human beings with their own rights. It differentiated
childhood from adulthood, defined it, and designated it as a special
developmental stage that involved dignity, growth, education, and rec-
reation (UNICEF, n.d.-b). The convention embraces several universal human rights, which assures several key principles and values, and
should guide efforts to prioritize children's rights and optimal development in the United States. The key principles and values include:

- Universality and inalienability: Human rights are
  universal and inalienable. All people everywhere in the
  world are entitled to them. No one can voluntarily give
  them up. Nor can others take them away.
- Indivisibility: Human rights are indivisible. Whether
  civil, political, economic, social, or cultural in nature, they
  are all inherent to the dignity of every human person.
  Consequently, they all have equal status as rights. There is
  no such thing as a 'small' right. There is no hierarchy of
  human rights.
- Interdependence and interrelatedness: the realization
  of one right often depends, wholly or in part, upon the
  realization of others. For instance, the realization of the
  right to health may depend on the realization of the right
  to education or of the right to information.
- Equality and non-discrimination: All individuals are
  equal as human beings and by virtue of the inherent
  dignity of each human person. All human beings are
  entitled to their human rights without discrimination of

any kind, such as race, color, sex, ethnicity, age, language, religion, political or other opinion, national or social origin, disability, property, birth, or other status as explained by the human rights treaty bodies.

- Participation and inclusion: Every person and all peoples are entitled to active, free and meaningful participation in, contribution to, and enjoyment of civil, political, economic, social, and cultural development, through which human rights and fundamental freedoms can be realized.
- Accountability and rule of law: States and other duty-bearers must comply with the legal norms and standards enshrined in human rights instruments. Where they fail to do so, aggrieved rights-holders are entitled to institute proceedings for appropriate redress before a competent court or other adjudicator, in accordance with the rules and procedures provided by law. (*UNICEF Finland, 2015*, as cited by UNICEF, n.d.-b)

In the United States, Walker et al. (1999) outlined two major orientations that inform the discussion around children's rights—the nurturance orientation and the self-determination orientation. The nurturance orientation assumes a paternalistic stance, presupposing that others in society (e.g., parents, government) know what is best for a child, and does not engage the child in the decision-making process. This orientation focuses on all the ills that affect children, such as poverty and abuse, and insists that children need to be protected from these concerns. While inherently the orientation values the essence of children, it treats children as objects that lack the capacity to judge and choose (Walker et al, 1999).

Conversely, the self-determination orientation prioritizes the child's right to choose. This orientation argues that children are entitled to the same rights as adults and can exercise these rights in various arenas, including their homes, schools, courts, and so on. For example, proponents of this orientation would contend that children should have the right to vote (Peterson, 1993).

Walker et al. (1999) propose striking a delicate balance between these two orientations to ensure children's rights for protection, entitlement, and self-determination. They recognize the benefits of each orientation and recommend starting with the nurturance orientation given the vulnerable nature of infants. But as children mature and develop decision-making competence, the self-determination orientation should be introduced to guide any and all matters affecting the child. Walker et al. (1999) recognize the family, guided by parents or caregivers, as the organizing unit responsible for these efforts. Hence, one key function of parents or caregivers is to foster the character development and human competence of their children. To ensure this they advocate for a national stance in the United States that could inform these efforts, so they maintain that ratifying the UN Convention on the Rights of the Child is a good first step toward recognizing, promoting, and guaranteeing children's rights in the home, school, community, and nation (Walker et al., 1999).

This Convention on the Rights of the Child and the related universal rights outlined above have been widely accepted by most of the world. While other countries have signed and ratified the Convention, the United States is the only country that has signed it but has refused to ratify it (Mehta, 2015), claiming the treaty would compromise its sovereignty, although it has signed other international treaties. Walker et al. (1999) argue that signing and ratifying the convention in the United States would be a good first step toward helping this country develop a national policy to promote children's rights. They characterize U.S. efforts around children's rights as a "patchwork of policies" that prevent protection, entitlement, and self-determination. Again, through a feminist lens, the refusal to ratify the treaty in the United States for the most vulnerable citizens is a direct consequence of a patriarchal social structure, which prioritizes and advances the protection and rights of some members in society over other members.

Child Maltreatment, Feminist Theory, and Intersectionality

One unique contribution of feminist theory is the notion of intersectionality (hooks, 2015). Intersectionality considers the interactions amongst the various aspects of one's identity (e.g., race, ethnicity, gender) as well as the multiple contexts (e.g., cultural, structural, economic) in which these identities are embedded (Howard & Renfrow, 2014). While intersectionality will be discussed further in chapter 2, the following vignette highlights a number of identity factors, including ethnicity, class, gender, and religion, that inform the conceptualization of this case. Again, a cursory review of this case might suggest physical abuse and possibly medical neglect; however, the religious ritual, informed by the family's cultural background, adds additional layers of complexity that warrants a more thoughtful analysis.

The Case of Marco. Marco showed up to school with his shoulders covered in bandages. He carried his backpack in his arms and requested assistance to put his backpack in his locker. His classroom teacher observed these behaviors and asked Marco if he was okay. Marco stated that he was fine. The teacher then patted Marco on his shoulder and Marco flinched in pain. Concerned, the teacher asked him what had happened, but Marco stated, "I can't tell you." The teacher became suspicious, so she inquired further. He confirmed, "I am not allowed to tell you." During Marco's Physical Education (PE) class, Marco was in the locker room changing into his PE uniform when one of the bandages came off. His PE teacher observed a fresh scar in a peculiar pattern. She thought to herself that this was not the typical scar of someone who had fallen. The scar appeared to form a small pattern on his shoulder. The PE teacher approached Marco and asked if someone did this to him. Marco nodded his head and again stated, "I am forbidden from telling you about this." The PE teacher consulted with his classroom teacher and they made a report to the Department of Children and Families. Upon investigation, it was revealed that Marco identified as an Afro-Caribbean, Cuban male who practiced a form of religion referred to as Palo. The scars on his shoulders were part of a sacred ritual of initiation. The scarification process was done by a religious leader who used the sharp bone of a sacrificed animal.

Case Discussion. The major type of potential child maltreatment associated with this case involves physical abuse, as the adults involved in this case engaged in behaviors that caused physical harm. Additionally, if the carving causes complications and is not properly treated, it may involve medical neglect. One question that arises from this case is whether the family's religious background absolves the parents of child maltreatment. As noted by the Pew Research Center, while all states have laws barring child maltreatment, at least thirty-four have exemptions in the civil child maltreatment statutes for child-focused, medical interventions that may conflict with a family's religious beliefs (Sandstrom, 2016). Additionally, some states include religious exemptions to criminal child abuse and neglect statutes. Finally, Marco's role and involvement in the ritual needs to be further understood. In the subsequent chapters, we will consider the core multicultural concepts as they relate to intersectionality and explore frameworks that highlight cultural strengths as well as optimal child maltreatment prevention and management.

Institutional Abuse: Expanding the Lens

Often times child maltreatment is associated primarily with parents or caregivers. However, institutions that are charged with protecting children can also engage in child maltreatment and there are social structures that indirectly or directly promote child maltreatment. Institutional abuse involves abuse and neglect that occurs in settings outside the home, such as schools, foster care, or detention centers (New Jersey Department of Children and Families, n.d.). When examining the ACYF 2019 data, one might assume that the rates of institutional abuse are low (less than 1%); however, we argue that there are numerous instances of sanctioned societal practices that meet the criteria for child maltreatment that go unquestioned, hence a need to broaden the definition of institutional abuse. To this end, we need to apply a lens that expands the focus and appreciates the influences of larger forces. Belsky's (1980) classic article, "Child Maltreatment: An Ecological Integration," offers a conceptual framework that captures the multiple external forces that are associated with child maltreatment. Adopting Bronfenbrenner's (1977) Ecological Systems theory, discussed earlier in this chapter, Belsky enumerates how larger social units engage in or contribute toward child maltreatment. Specifically, he highlights how parental unemployment or underemployment, limited support systems, higher rates of violence in the United States, "children as property" sentiments, and "pro-spanking" attitudes lead to abuse and neglect. This section examines larger structures that engage promote behaviors that meet the criteria for child maltreatment.

Recently, the American Psychological Association (Gershoff, 2021) sponsored a congressional briefing supporting the *Protecting Our Students in Schools Act*. This bill, endorsed by dozens of prominent organizations, would require the banning of corporal punishment in schools in order to qualify for federal funding. To date, nineteen schools allow the use of corporal punishment as a form of discipline (APA, 2021b), despite its disturbing impact. According to Gershoff

(2021), this practice in schools, which we deem to be government-sanctioned violence and a form of institutional abuse, "causes both physical and psychological injury, is ineffective in promoting positive student behavior, interferes with student learning, is used disproportionally with some groups of students more than others, and creates a negative school climate" (1). Most physical disciplining occurs with a wooden paddle and leads to physical injury, such as welts, bruises, and broken bones, and emotional distress (Gershoff et al, 2015). Gershoff (2021) observed that if this same action was used with adults, the paddle would be considered a weapon and the act an assault; yet when it happens to children it is simply characterized as discipline.

Later in this book, we also discuss the cruel and sad practice conducted by the U.S. Government in 2018 with immigrant families arriving at our Southern border, where children were separated from their parents. The Human Rights Watch, a non-profit organization that monitors abuses across the world, captured the horrific accounts of these victims, noting that this forced separation led to their traumatization (Bochenech, 2019). Specifically, the children interviewed reported chronic anxiety, concentration difficulties, sleepless nights, and mood shifts—all classic signs of trauma. The APA (2018) called this government-sanctioned practice "needless and cruel," and they urged the administration to rescind the separation policy, warning that it could lead to negative outcomes for these children, including arrested development, academic difficulties, and psychological distress. Despite it being authorized by the government, this practice amounts to neglect and psychological maltreatment.

Finally, as we write this book, there is a national controversy around children returning to schools in the midst of the new and highly contagious Delta variant of COVID-19. While the CDC is advising taking numerous precautions, at least eight states have banned schools from enforcing a mask mandate (Speakman, 2021). Given the evolving nature of this pandemic and the many unknowns, we assert that these states are being careless and neglectful, and if left unchallenged would be engaging in child maltreatment. If the situation was reversed, and parents were placing children in imminent danger, they would be investigated and charged with neglect. Yet this government-sanctioned practice of neglect could go unexamined, unquestioned, and unpunished. Other problematic government-sanctioned policies practiced against BIPOC children, families, and communities are also discussed in our other volumes (Calzada et al., forthcoming; Phillips et al., forthcoming; Ross et al., forthcoming).

Several scholars have appreciated how ongoing advocacy can shape public opinion, ensure accountability, foster legal reforms, and promote optimal public policies (Belsky, 1980; Gershoff & Bitensky, 2007; Walker et al., 1999). This was certainly the case with domestic violence. Gershoff and Bitensky (2007) observed that powerful advocacy, fueled by feminists, led to several significant developments, including anti-violence attitudes toward women, the creation of shelters, and legal reforms in local, state, and federal arenas. Similar developments occurred in Sweden, the first country to ban corporal punishment in 1983; as a result of the ban, the country enjoyed several positive outcomes. As discussed by Gershoff and Bitensky (2007), subsequent to the ban public opinion shifted away from the physical punishment of children; the incidence of child abuse decreased; injuries associated with physical assaults lessened; and youth violence and delinquency declined.

Yet children remain the only class of individuals in the United Sates that we can still legally strike; if we physically strike an adult, there will be legal recourses and consequences. If we are truly committed to ending child maltreatment, we must actively engage in comprehensive and extensive advocacy that prioritizes children's optimal development, stops abuse, and communicates to the public that all violence toward youth is deplorable. This principle of advocacy, promoted by Goodman et al. (2004), is discussed further throughout this book, especially in chapter 4.

Closing Summary

Child maltreatment is a major public health concern in the United States and is associated with numerous negative outcomes. Additionally, certain groups are affected disproportionately by child maltreatment. When considered through a feminist lens, it becomes evident that patriarchal elements can play a key role in contributing toward and maintaining child maltreatment. Understanding various cultural beliefs, values, and strengths can be key to wellness and prevention. The next chapter introduces and examines key multicultural core concepts and explores how they relate to the basis, prevention, and management of child maltreatment.

2

Core Multicultural Concepts

In diversity, there is beauty and
there is strength.
—Maya Angelou

Every individual exists within a larger context of intersecting identities and systems. Norms of healthy and maladaptive parenting behavior particularly depend upon cultural background (APA, 2017b; Bronfenbrenner, 1977; Hays, 2001). While laws and regulations at both state and national levels seek to clarify what constitutes abuse, they may fail to address these internal cultural expectations and systemic factors. These factors impact both the act of maltreatment and the context in which it arose. In this light, it is essential to utilize an ecosystemic model in order to effectively address and prevent maltreatment. This chapter provides an overview of factors that impact different dimensions of identity. Feminist and systemic approaches serve as grounding frameworks, both for the present chapter and also for understanding child maltreatment more broadly. And finally, we review the cases discussed in chapter 1 with an additional application of a multicultural lens of analysis.

Feminist Approach

As discussed previously, when addressing child maltreatment, it is particularly salient to understand the historical context for clinical interventions, including ways in which institutions have historically reinforced problematic patterns of oppression. No field of research or practice can be viewed independently from the societal structures from which it emerged. The foundations for the conceptualization and treatment of mental illness include elements of pathologization and disempowerment that long negated the experiences of women and people of color. Psychology itself has historically been "dominated by male theory, research and practice," as "feminist psychologists argued that Freud's theories, such as 'penis envy' and hysteria, were gender biased" (Draganović, 2011, 112). Of note, feminist therapy first emerged in the 1960s in response to both external sources of oppression and internal failure within the field of psychology to adequately address the needs of women.* In contrast, the goal of feminist therapy is to impart "transformation and social change in daily personal life, and in relationships with the social, emotional and political environments" (Brown, 1994, 22). In the case of child maltreatment, disrupting maladaptive systems that lead to perpetuation of abuse and harm is essential to imparting lasting change. For example, in the case of Miguelina, noting the deep family history of intimate partner violence and subsequent child maltreatment is essential for ending maladaptive patterns of intergenerational trauma. Understanding the larger social and cultural contexts that contribute to these patterns will help determine the appropriate interventions.

As Brown (2018) notes, "therapy as usual operating in the absence of an analysis of gender and power, practiced in ways that can actively or inadvertently uphold problematic status quos and reinforce hierarchies of value inherent in dominant cultures can enable systemic forms of oppression" (124). In the case of Amelia, her mother gave her a *tapa boca* after Amelia rolled her eyes and used profanity. By considering the value of *respeto,* a provider takes into consideration the importance of obedience and the respect given to adults in Latino

---

*For more on the historical origins and shifts within the movement, please see Brown, L. S. (2018), *Feminist Therapy* (Washington, DC: American Psychological Association).

families. Failing to include this value, which is meant to maintain family harmony, in the overall analysis of the situation results in an overemphasis of the Western values of independence and autonomy (Calzada et al., 2010).

In another example that incorporates feminist theory, Brown (2010) suggests that in the case of a woman who was sexually abused as a child, dissociative symptoms may in fact be protective mechanisms (286). Further, providing appropriate supports for an individual in crisis is contingent on understanding external forces of oppression that may in turn lead to negative consequences. Indeed, individuals and even whole families or communities may internalize oppression, leading to a variety of negative health outcomes (Moane, 2003). In contrast, research has begun to show that the process of ethnic-racial socialization, in which families purposefully teach their children about the values and customs important to their specific cultural identity, is associated with positive child outcomes (Caughy et al., 2006; Caughy et al., 2002). In order to effectively understand, treat, and empower individuals who have been oppressed, feminist theory highlights the importance of understanding that symptoms may in fact be adaptive responses to a perpetual cycle of oppression or the result of intergenerational trauma.

Sadly, women and girls experience a disproportionate degree of violence as compared to men. Women of color are more likely to be raped or physically assaulted than their White counterparts (Tjaden & Thoennes, 2000). Individuals who are victims of violence as children are also more likely to experience victimization as adults (Tjaden & Thoennes, 2000). Additionally, previous researchers have highlighted the overlap between incidents of domestic violence or observation of marital discord and child maltreatment within families (Hamby et al., 2010; Osofsky, 2003). Recognizing the overlap between various types of violence and victimization highlights patterns within families and communities. Incorporating an additional systemic approach may be particularly helpful for identifying intergenerational trauma while simultaneously expanding the cultural context for maltreatment behaviors.

Systems Approach

Understanding individual functioning, including the unique relationships within families, necessitates an integrative model in which intersecting aspects of identity are addressed holistically, as they relate to child maltreatment (Fontes, 2005). This model includes incorporating and understanding factors within individuals, between persons, and external forces that shape behavior. As noted in chapter 1, an ecological model was introduced by Bronfenbrenner (1977) to highlight the importance of external environmental factors on individual functioning. This theory posits that context matters, particularly the complex interplay of relationships, systemic influences, and larger cultural forces. As noted in chapter 1, specific forces include five tiers of influence, including: 1) *microsystems*: interactions between an individual and others; 2) *mesosystems*: interactions between microsystems; 3) *exosystems*: indirect sources of influence; 4) *macrosystems:* larger cultural forces as well as external; and 5) *chronosystems:* changes over time (Bronfenbrenner, 1977).

In the case of Bashiir, there is a larger macrosystemic focus on compulsory attendance in education. Viewed through a westernized, unidimensional approach to treatment, Bashiir's parents are not fulfilling their obligation to send their child to school. As mandated by state laws, children in all states of the United States are expected to attend public school. Compulsory educational laws were first introduced in Massachusetts in the 1600s by the Puritan settlers (Katz, 1976). These laws were intended to limit neglect of children, to ensure adequate training for the workforce, and to ensure standards of religious achievement. Standards have shifted dramatically in the subsequent years regarding the content of education, but the compulsory mandate remains. A majority of states require students to attend school between the ages of 6 and 18, with slight age deviations depending on state. Exceptions may be made for home schooling. Viewed from this perspective, Bashiir's family is not complying with their legal mandate. However, this understanding also excludes the specific context of Bashiir's own family and culture. Further, using a multisystemic intervention, as recommended by Boyd-Franklin (2003), allows for comprehensive interventions that support the clients, their families, and their communities simultaneously. Utilizing an overly compressed lens eliminates valuable opportunities to fully understand a client or family system's experiences.

The *Multicultural Guidelines* adopted by the American Psychological Association's Council of Representatives (APA, 2017b) build on an ecological model to focus on factors that impact the interactions between individuals and the professionals with whom they interact, including five levels of influence. These layers include: 1) *self-definition*, individuals within a particular relationship; 2) *community*, or school and family context; 3) *institutional impact on engagement*, comprised of external systems such as the legal, mental health, state, federal, and educational systems; 4) *domestic and international climate*, including societal context and specific human rights; and 5), *outcomes*, results of the interactions between the parties identified in level one (APA, 2017b). Within relationships, every individual presents a unique array of identities that influence their expectations, values, and responses to others.

Expanding the view to include this larger context allows for discussion of other factors that may affect Bashiir and his family. Based on the data supplied by the caseworker, it is unclear if the family is documented or not. Additionally, it would be helpful to determine the family's familiarity with U.S. customs prior to their arrival in the country and their level of acculturation in order to better understand their context (Berry, 2005). The family may not be able or may not feel secure enough to seek support through immigration support services. Refugee and asylee families may have a healthy fear of approaching official channels for support, as this may lead to questions about their residency and potential deportation. Bashiir and his family may have made the choice to focus on resources within the family in order to limit the possibility that an external support would share information about the family with others. It would be problematic for a clinician to focus solely on the legal mandate for school attendance, rather than identifying or addressing the cultural familial expectations and context. Viewing the family's behavior as atypical, problematic, or incorrect discounts potential opportunities for cultural humility (Gallardo, 2014) and further amplifies the sense of the client as an "other" or an outsider to the "correct" cultural code (Hook et al., 2013).

Individual Identity

Starting at the individual level, it is important to note that identity is complex, representing a combination of static and evolving elements that create a more complex whole (Fuentes & Adamés, 2011). In order to better understand factors that impact families and that underlay patterns of child maltreatment, it is essential to first develop a foundational context. Viewed independently, any one characteristic provides only a unidimensional and therefore incomplete understanding of one's self. Hays (2001) proposed the ADDRESSING multidimensional framework of identity to encapsulate a range of identifiers, including: age and generational influences, developmental disability, disability acquired later in life, religion and spiritual orientation, ethnicity, socioeconomic status, sexual orientation, indigenous heritage, national origin, and gender. Within these various identities, it is also critical to avoid the trap of "ethnic glossing," or oversimplification of any one identifier (APA, 2017b; Trimble & Dickson, 2005). Reducing an entire group of individuals to one homogenous stereotype is an oversight and potentially may lead to more significant ramifications related to mental health (Yoo et al., 2010). This section discusses concepts relevant to individual identity, including acculturation, ethnic-racial socialization, racial identity, microaggressions, institutional racism, and intersectionality.

Racial Identity

Racial identity is an aspect of individual identity that "one forms as a member of a racial or ethnic group" (Sue & Sue, 2016, 764). As a country, the United States has made advances in the awareness of racial identity. However, more needs to be done to address the inequities people of color face in all aspects of American life. According to Neville and Awad (2014), denying the realities people of color experience regarding racism and discrimination exacerbates disparities and unjust treatment. An example of this is for someone to adopt a "color-blind" point of view. Color blindness, as this is commonly referred to in the literature, neglects the experiences people of color face. Instead, taking a color-conscious approach toward interactions with others and confronting the complexities of race is a step towards reducing inequality and the mistreatment of people of color (Neville & Awad, 2014).

There are multiple models of racial identity theory. Many of these theories include multiple stages or categories. Early racial identity theories for people of color sought to examine intra-racial conflict, but associated assertive traits with aggression (Vontress, 1971). These initial models did not identify racial minority individuals' pride in racial identity as a norm of healthy development, and further placed blame on Black clients for rifts in therapeutic relationships with White clinicians. In contrast, later models, such as the Nigrescence Racial Identity Model, equated the process of "becoming black" as a healthy norm (Cross et al., 1991). Racial identity theory indicates that individuals progress through specific stages of identity development related to both internal cognition and external social forces (Sue & Sue, 2012). Knowing one's own racial identity is a process that involves introspection, willingness to engage in difficult conversations, and honest appraisal of one's own beliefs (Helms, 2018).

Of note, racial identity involves elements of one's external culture. Bashiir, as a first-generation immigrant, may experience his own racial identity differently than a U.S.–born individual who identifies as Black. Identifying an individual's specific state of racial identity may provide insight into their internal sense of worth and their potential response to external interventions, particularly by individuals from backgrounds that diverge from their own. This notion is particularly salient in the context of child maltreatment as families of color are often in contact with practitioners or members of law enforcement that the families may associate with sources of systemic oppression. For example, Bashiir's family lives in an area where there is a high level of gang activity. It would be important to assess the family's level of comfort with and perceptions of local law enforcement and other agencies with authority (e.g., child protective services).

Institutional Racism

Larger external systems of oppression, such as institutional racism, may also impact families' overall well-being and mental health. Institutional racism includes the social and structural policies that oppress people of color with standards specific to them that create unequal access to opportunities and services. Institutional racism has furthered discriminatory practices around economic opportunities, healthcare, and other institutions, resulting in forced acculturation of people of color (Sue & Sue, 2016). This discrimination then has an adverse impact on the mental and physical health of these individuals (Saleem & Lambert, 2016). According to Saleem and Lambert (2016), institutional discrimination impacts the quality of schools, neighborhoods, parents' employment status, and even the quality of one's home. Institutional racism includes practices inscribed within larger social systems. For example, the practice of "redlining" within real estate entails limiting Black and Brown people's access to purchasing homes within specific geographic areas. Owning a home can increase access to equity, school systems, economic opportunity, and transportation (Szto, 2013). But the federal government, banks, and real estate agencies have historically limited Black and Brown people's access to obtaining loans and purchasing homes in White suburban neighborhoods. Redlining often originates from multiple sources, with problematic or sub-prime bank loans, real estate agents fraudulently telling people of color who are prospective buyers that a home has sold, and homeowners refusing to sell to clients based on their race (Szto, 2013). There is a complex relationship between violence and poverty, with lack of economic resources both limiting options for escaping violence and increasing susceptibility for intimate partner violence and child maltreatment (Gibbs et al., 2017; Goodman et al., 2009).

In all of the cases discussed in chapter 1, context is important. Bashiir's and Jaquann's families live in environments in which they are subject to neighborhood and community violence. Amelia's family does not have access to adequate interpreters. Marco's teachers may not have had any exposure to or knowledge about his religious identity. Both Bashiir and Amelia are first generation immigrants, and all of the cases involve racial and ethnic minorities. In the United States, nearly 58 percent of hate crimes are committed against individuals based on their race, ethnicity, or ancestry, and 20 percent due to bias about religion (Federal Bureau of Investigation [FBI], 2019). Providing comprehensive supports for any of these children and for their families necessitates a thorough examination of any additional external factors that negatively impact their functioning. This builds on the APA's guidelines for integrating community into comprehensive interventions (APA, 2017b).

Acculturation

For individuals who immigrate to the United States, there are a variety of potential responses to leaving one environment and transitioning to another environment. Berry proposed a model of acculturation, defined as "the dual process of cultural and psychological change that takes place as a result of contact between two or more cultural groups and their individual members" (Berry, 2005, 698). Individuals may experience tension between disparate identities and cultures, at times feeling "strung between cultures, strung between identities" (Singer & Tummala-Narra, 2013, 294). Immigrants may adopt the culture of their new environment or *assimilate*. They may also choose to maintain the culture of their country of origin, limiting changes regardless of their new environment, termed *separation*. Immigrants may also reject both cultures through a process of *marginalization*. At times, identities may feel more in harmony. *Integration* represents a stage of incorporating aspects of the country of origin and the new environment, thereby creating a unique composite that includes elements of both. Different family members may acculturate in different ways, thereby causing potential tension within families (APA, 2013; Falicov, 2012). Addressing this aspect of identity is an ethical mandate for clinicians (Singer & Fuentes, 2018). Further, level of acculturation may directly intersect with themes of child maltreatment when traditional cultural values appear to clash with legal mandates for reporting.

In the case of Miguelina, it would be very helpful to assess each individual family member's level of acculturation. This evaluation may help determine the family's level of openness and comfort talking to individuals outside of the family. Establishing trust is an essential element of obtaining accurate information about potential child maltreatment. Further, it may help to understand how cultural norms impact the process of reporting maltreatment. Identifying the family's level of acculturation would further assist in assessing their viewpoints on appropriate versus inappropriate physical contact and obtaining information about family history of abuse.

Shifting to the case of Marco, the scarification ritual practiced by Marco and his family is very complex. Legally, scarification rituals of minors are considered a form of physical abuse in the United States. However, Marco's spiritual following of Palo views scarification as critical in his becoming a man. As noted in the *Multicultural Guidelines*, stage of life and development overlay psychosocial and cultural practices (APA, 2017b). Many cultures have prescribed rituals for honoring or marking the transition from child to adult. According to the family, scarification is necessary to protect Marco and ensure his becoming a man. However, the American Academy of Pediatrics calls for the repeal of religious exemptions amongst all states to ensure protection under the law of all children (American Academy of Pediatrics, Committee on Bioethics, 2013). As a result, some states have repealed their religious exemption of child abuse. It may also be helpful to note the tension between cultural practices that identify Marco as transitioning to the status of adult with his legal status as a minor.

It may be helpful to openly discuss these conflicting viewpoints with the family.

This standpoint impacts Marco's community given that it increases the vulnerability of families who engage in spiritual rituals with their children. Additionally, Marco's religious identity of Palo may make him and his family more of a target given that his religion has been depicted as a form of "black magic" and Santeria in news and social media venues. Overall, the report to child protectives services has resulted in extreme distress within Marco's community, family members, his spiritual leaders, and himself. Once again, the interaction between clinician and client who have very different cultural backgrounds and worldviews may pose a problem in limiting conversation about the ways in which culture impacts expectations for family roles and safety.

Ethnic-Racial Socialization

Themes of acculturation may also overlap with a family's level of ethnic-racial socialization. Within families, an individual's racial identity may be shaped by many factors, including micro-level interactions with parents and caregivers. Ethnic-racial socialization is the transmission of information about race and ethnicity from adults to children (Hughes et al., 2006). More specifically, ethnic-racial socialization involves the ways minority individuals are taught to navigate what it means to be of a certain racial and ethnic group through the messages received from their parental figures. Ethnic and racially diverse parents transmit messages that impart values related to issues such as cultural identity, racial pride, group social status, intergroup relations, language abilities, and phenotypic characteristics. These processes may include handing down cultural traditions through modeling and instruction or teaching their children about histories of their racial or ethnic group. For instance, in the case of Marco, the sacred ritual of scarification is a cultural tradition passed down through the generations in an effort to protect and celebrate the individual.

Parents also discuss with their families the prevalence of stereotypes, potential discrimination they may face, and ways to cope with this discrimination in hopes of preparing their children for the roles ethnic and racial identity will play in their lives (Hughes et al., 2006; White-Johnson et al., 2010). Hughes and his colleagues described ethnic and racial socialization as "psychologists' efforts to understand how families of color experience and discuss social inequalities and injustices and how they teach children to manage them" (Hughes et al., 2006, 748). As mental health professionals attempt to assess and treat child maltreatment, they should understand the ethnic-racial socialization messages parents transmit to their children and how this relates to the family's and the individual's overall functioning. Further, it is necessary for clinicians to recognize how their own identity may impact interventions they authorize, including when they inadvertently utilize an ethnocentric approach that negates their clients' cultural reality (Fontes, 2005).

In the case of Marco, it is necessary to understand the context of both the family's level of acculturation and their ethnic-racial socialization. Specifically, there was a lack of communication from Marco as to what happened to him (i.e., he would simply say he could not say). Marco's refusal to inform his teachers of what happened is part of the families' ethnic-racial socialization in that he was respecting his parents' and elders' message about the sacredness of the ritual. In cases of child maltreatment, incidents identified as abuse in one context may be construed as cultural norms in another context (Raman & Hodes, 2012).

Hughes et al.'s (2006) review of research on racial socialization found that the degree to which parents discuss bias might vary. African American parents are more likely to seek to prepare their children to face potential future discrimination. In order to protect their children, parents of color may engage in an adaptive "promotion of mistrust" (Hughes et al., 2006, 757), thereby warning their children to limit information shared with those from different backgrounds. For historically marginalized groups, this practice developed out of necessity. Racial minority parents are more likely to warn their sons about discrimination than their daughters, alter their messages according to children's developmental ages, and encourage practicing traditions from the family's country of origin (Hughes et al., 2006).

A clinician's own ethnic-racial socialization may also impact their ability to appropriately identify instances of child maltreatment. "As the National Research Council has noted, assaults of children by their parents tend to go unrecognized because they are socially construed as discipline rather than violence" (Tjaden & Thoennes, 2000, 36). Practitioners may be reluctant to label a behavior as aggressive due to their own fears that it is not their responsibility to differentiate between cultural expectations and child maltreatment, or due to concerns that they are applying harmful stereotypes about the client's cultural identity (Raman & Hodes, 2012).

Microaggressions

There are additional sources of oppression that may impact internal familial stress and subsequent response to external interventions. Specifically, microaggressions are verbal, behavioral, or environmental messages that "communicate hostile, derogatory, or negative racial slights and insults towards people of color" (Sue et al., 2007, 271). Microaggressions may be intentional or unintentional, with the latter being more often the case. There are three forms of microaggressions. These may include the use of derogatory language, such as identifying an individual of Asian descent as "Oriental," or denying someone access to a certain venue solely based upon their skin tone. It is also crucial to note that microaggressions can occur within the context of therapy itself (Miles et al., 2021). While Sue et al. (2007) indicate that microassaults are often privately expressed, they may become more overt threats or insults if the individual expressing the assault either feels that they will not be penalized for doing so, or commits a "slip" and inadvertently expresses internal thoughts.

Microinsults are subtly rude and insensitive messages regarding one's racial identity (Sue et al., 2007). These interactions may start with questions about how a person of color was able to achieve a position or gain access to a coveted spot at a university (e.g., "Why do you think you were promoted rather than [White colleague]?"). While the individual communicating the message might be unaware of its impact, the recipient will experience a degree of harm. The impact of these statements may include an assumption that the individual should not have received this promotion or is not qualified for the position. Critiques of affirmative action may fall into this category if they assume that the only reason an individual was accepted or promoted was due to their race rather than their skills or qualifications.

Microinvalidations are messages that negate the experiences, thoughts, and feelings of people of color (Sue et al., 2007). For example, asking a person of color where they are "from" and not accepting that the individual's birthplace was the United States is a microinvalidation. Rather, a person might assume that individuals who are Asian American were born outside of the United States, "conveying the message that they are perpetual foreigners in their own land" (DeAngelis, 2009, para. 19). Microaggressions are difficult to address, as Sue notes:

> It's a monumental task to get White people to realize that they are delivering microaggressions, because it's scary to them.... It assails their self-image of being good, moral, decent human beings to realize that maybe at an unconscious level they have biased thoughts, attitudes and feelings that harm people of color (DeAngelis, 2009, para. 7).

Microaggressions occur not only in the daily interactions of people, but also in the policies, structures, and institutions of society. This may complicate interventions if the microaggressions come from individuals in positions of power, including practitioners intervening in cases of suspected child maltreatment. Clinicians' own cultural identities and biases may lead them to identify some behaviors as harmful based on the family's cultural context or to oversimplify an entire racial group thereby ignoring important nuances within cultures (Raman & Hodes, 2012). These transgressions, if not monitored, are bound to affect the assessment and treatment of child abuse and neglect.

Individuals who immigrate to the United States may particularly experience microaggressions when they are asked "Where are you from?" or told to "Speak English." In the case of Amelia, it is quite likely that she has had the experience of spending time with her parents in a public setting in which they were speaking Spanish. Some youth may internalize negative views about their country of origin or about family members who maintain traditional practices. Amelia may also experience some of this tension and may be the recipient of microaggressions due to her frequent role as her parents' interpreter. In chapter 4, we discuss microinterventions, a set of strategies for responding to microaggressions.

Intersectionality

As noted in chapter 1, no one element of identity exists in a vacuum; rather, all elements of an individual's identity overlap, creating a composite and comprising a whole self. Crenshaw (1989) coined the term "intersectionality" to address the unique experiences of Black women in facing a unique brand of discrimination that resulted from the combination of both their gender and their racial identities. Understanding the interplay between these two identities is essential, "because the intersectional experience is greater than the sum of racism and sexism, any analysis that does not take intersectionality into account cannot sufficiently address the particular manner in which Black women are subordinated" (Crenshaw, 1989, 140). Crenshaw originally applied this concept to a lawsuit against General Motors that focused on potential discrimination within the company against Black women. "Evidence adduced at trial revealed that General Motors simply did not hire Black women prior to 1964 and that all of the Black women hired after 1970 lost their jobs in a seniority-based layoff during a subsequent recession" (Crenshaw, 1989, 141). Because the company did hire White women and Black men, the court ruling indicated that no discrimination had taken place. However, Crenshaw argued that the experience of Black women and their treatment within the company was unique, and subsequently should be examined separately. The concept of intersectionality has been broadened to consider how a person's socio-cultural factors (e.g., race, gender, sexual orientation) interact to inform each other, leading to the enhancement, neutralization, or diminishment of identity factors (Fuentes & Adamés, 2011). Turning to the case of Amelia, a Western perspective that emphasizes independence and autonomy may suggest that the mother was encouraging gender specific roles by expecting Amelia to clean and tend to the home. However, taking in to account the value of *respeto* allows further understanding of the role that Latino mothers play in instilling and preserving cultural values and customs. For example, this may include an open conversation with both Amelia and her parents about their expectations for communication within the family. It is possible to integrate adaptive expectations for respecting elders with advocating for increasing autonomy.

Similarly, in the case of Miguelina, the client may have learned similar norms for respecting authority. In addition to identifying with her family's country of origin and her ethnicity, she also identifies as female. In her family, messages about gender are very clear. Specifically, her father's use of derogatory terms to describe women and his dismissal of Miguelina's self-worth (e.g., telling her she will never amount to anything) are bound to inform her gender identity. These factors combined may contribute to a sense that Miguelina's voice, perspectives, and experiences are secondary to those of her male family members. This may impact her willingness to speak about her abuse, particularly if she believes that it will contribute to negative outcomes for her family, retribution from her father, or both.

Utilizing a more integrated, and therefore more thorough, understanding of a client's multiple and intersecting identities is both an ethical imperative and a cultural competency. The *Multicultural Guidelines* suggest that understanding intersectionality is a key element of both understanding and potentially changing inequitable systems. The guidelines assert the following:

> By recognizing that an individual's identity is derived from interacting systemic effects, psychologists strive to understand associated human biases informed by systems of power, privilege, oppression, social dictates, constraints, values, and negative perceptions of marginalized societies (APA, 2017b).

Conversely, implementing a unidimensional, linear approach to identity may emphasize patriarchal or heteronormative systems (Shin, 2015). Using this more comprehensive analytic lens allows clinicians addressing child maltreatment to incorporate both aspects of resilience associated with a client's identity, and potential risk factors for exposure to violence and oppression.

Integrating Aspects of Individual Identity

Additional consideration of overall family stressors necessitates recognition that maintaining the wellbeing of multiple children in a family may depend on the parents maintaining their employment. Education may become a lower priority if the family needs to make difficult choices about basic needs such as housing and food to support the entire family system. In the case of Bashiir, within the family's cultural unit Bashiir, as the oldest, may be considered of age to take on shared responsibility for his younger siblings. Maturity may be a socially constructed concept, with divergent views about the transitional age between child and adult depending on one's culture. Traumatic or difficult circumstances may also elicit protective instincts and parentification of older siblings. When making a diagnosis, clinicians should assess for the level of distress and impairment of the child to determine how problematic a behavior may be. In the case of Miguelina, her family does not appear to identify her brother's behavior as problematic, attempting to address the abuse discreetly. This may impact their willingness to participate in further treatment. In Bashiir's case, his parentified role (e.g., when a youth is expected to take on roles or responsibilities typically allocated to caregivers, such as childcare) is impairing him in that it prevents him from being able to go to school. It would also be helpful to discuss whether he (or his family) have concerns about this role. Fostering understanding of the family's cultural norms would create opportunities for conversation, collaboration, and partnership with the family in a more feminist and egalitarian manner (Brown, 2010; Goodman et al., 2004).

Approaching Child Protective Services about this issue, while potentially defensible from a legal standpoint, ignores potential opportunities to foster a collaborative and empowering approach. In the case of Bashiir, the therapist did end up meeting with the community elders and was able to find a time that parents were also available to come to the session. While the community elders reprimanded the parents for not asking for help sooner, they were also able to mobilize a network of other Somali refugee families in order to create a patchwork of adult supervision for Bashiir's younger siblings so that Bashiir could attend school. This dovetails with a multi-systems approach of including community or "non-blood kin" in conceptualization and interventions (Boyd-Franklin, 2013). This approach recognizes community supports as a form of resilience by tapping into existing resources to resolve the issue (APA, 2017b) without silencing the family's voice or undermining cultural expectations for proper channels (Goodman et al., 2004). Utilizing an intervention that addresses both the family's need for support and the child's ability to attend school is a key example of a culturally adaptive and integrative approach to treatment (APA, 2017b).

Relational Factors

Particularly in the context of child maltreatment, it is paramount to understand the factors that impact interpersonal interactions between individuals or family members. Similar to aspects of individual identity, every interaction between individuals is deeply impacted by their respective contexts and histories. These overlapping and intersecting identities are "cultural borderlands," specific "zones of similarity and differences between cultures [that] give rise to internal consistencies, conflicts, and contradictions as well as commonalities and resonances among groups and individuals" (Anzaldúa, 2012; Falicov, 2013, 14).

Navigating these shared and divergent identities necessitates a degree of self-awareness and reflexivity about one's own identity and its impact on a relationship with another individual (Singer & Tummala-Narra, 2013). In the case of Amelia, the mother and daughter dyad is experiencing relational tensions as a result of Amelia acquiring a cultural attitude typical of the dominant culture's teenage population. This dynamic affects Amelia's relationship with her mother, which results in tension within the family. Therefore, Amelia's mother, guided by her cultural values, perceives her daughter's attitude as disagreeable. Thus, Amelia's mother responds to her daughter's change in behavior by relying on her own cultural values and culturally appropriate behavior of *tapa boca*. When Child Protective Services (CPS) becomes involved, Amelia's family experiences an imbalance of power that challenges the parent's cultural beliefs about disciplining children.

Equally impactful is the interplay of power and privilege within a relationship or between groups of individuals. Privilege represents an inherent inequity often reinforced by systemic and interpersonal patterns (McIntosh, 1989). This imbalance in power may not be consciously sought, but represents an unearned advantage (Hays, 2001; McIntosh, 1989). Challenges related to power disparities may further result in conflict, tension, or additional relational crises (APA, 2017b; Singer & Tummala-Narra, 2013). It is also imperative to note that all aspects of identity, including the nature of privilege, are ever-adapting phenomena. The APA 2017 *Multicultural Guidelines* refer to these potential shifts as a dynamic process of fluidity (APA, 2017b). Identities and relationships may change and adapt over time. Additionally, an individual may experience relative privilege in one context but experience restrictions of a lower power group in another context. For example, in the case of Amelia, her mother may experience power within the family system as a matriarch, but she experiences a restriction of power when CPS determines that the mother's act of *tapa boca* was a form of child maltreatment.

Theoretical Frameworks for Intervention

Understanding and managing the complexities of individual identity, relational factors, and systemic influences represents an intensive and ongoing process. In order to understand and adequately respond to these factors, Sue and Sue (2012) assert that clinicians must engage in multiple processes, including: 1) fostering awareness of potential biases and internal value systems; 2) maintaining knowledge of the various identities and sources of influence that impact relationships; and 3) implementing effective skills and techniques that are tailored to specific situations. Further, identifying the specific role that a clinician may play depends upon various external and internal drivers, including the goal of the professional relationships, the client's locus of control (internal or external), and the client's level of acculturation (high or low) (Atkinson et al., 1993). Depending on the level of each of these elements, different goals and responsibilities are warranted. The next section further reviews specific multicultural and feminist guidelines that could serve as the foundation for interventions in cases of child maltreatment.

APA Multicultural Guidelines as Foundation for Conceptualization

The APA *Multicultural Guidelines* (APA, 2017b) emphasize that in order to better serve diverse populations and ensure culturally congruent assessments and interventions, practitioners must consider the following critical aspects:

1. Identity is fluid—multiple identities intersect.
2. Clinicians must acknowledge their own identities, as they might impact clinical and professional roles.
3. Communication and language impact relationships.
4. External social and systemic factors impact individual functioning.
5. Historical contexts of oppression and privilege shape lives, especially for minority individuals.
6. Clinicians have a mandate to utilize interventions and tools that are culturally adaptive.
7. A global lens is necessary for work conducted both abroad and within the United States.
8. Life stages and one's personal development impact functioning and overlap with biological, psychological, and social factors.
9. All interventions (research, clinical, etc.) must be carefully selected to ensure that they are culturally appropriate.
10. Utilizing an approach that is strengths-based is essential to enhance resilience.

Implementing these recommendations necessitates that clinicians identify gaps in their knowledge and seek appropriate training and consultation as well as identify appropriate referral resources when necessary. These approaches also may indicate that existing interventions and assessment measures developed for a westernized population will either need to be adapted or rejected in favor of evidence-based strategies that allow for the inclusion of differing cultural norms. Beyond engaging in a culturally sensitive manner with clients, clinicians must also identify and address inequitable differences in power between themselves and their clients. For instance, spiritual scarification as in the case of Marco, when viewed from a U.S.–based perspective, devalues the cultural significance of this ritual. Therefore, adhering to the recommendations and guidelines provided above will enhance not only the clinician's multicultural competency, but will help other professionals who work in the child maltreatment arena as well. The subsequent chapters consider these guidelines as they relate to the assessment and management of child maltreatment.

Feminism as a Call to Action

In addition to serving as a foundation for conceptualizing behaviors and understanding the impact of external factors, feminist approaches also provide a framework for working to impart change. Feminist approaches share roots with liberation psychology, which aims to ally the clinician with members of oppressed groups by "standing alongside them, working with them, seeking to develop collaborative relations that recognize power inequities (Comas-Diaz et al., 1998, 779). Further empowerment of individuals entails a shift for the clinician from expert to collaborator. Goodman et al. (2004) outline a series of principles building upon feminist ideology for effectively imparting change. In order to act as an agent of social justice, clinicians must: 1) engage in ongoing internal self-examination; 2) share power with their clients; 3) give clients an opportunity to express their own opinions, views, and experiences; 4) increase awareness and "raise consciousness"; 5) utilize a strengths-based approach; and 6) ensure that clients have tools to continue social change after the therapeutic relationship has ended. Applying these tools necessitates first understanding the external systemic factors that either promote or inhibit healthy functioning. These strategies and their application to child maltreatment management will be considered further in the subsequent chapters.

Additional Strategies for Systemic Change

There are multiple additional strategies that aim to both identify and address inequitable systems that might underlie child maltreatment. Specifically, social justice (Goodman et al., 2004), liberation theory (Freire, 1993), critical race theory (Ladson-Billing & Tate, 1995), and action research (Brydon-Miller et al., 2003) all identify potential problematic systemic dynamics and propose strategies for dismantling harmful patterns of behavior. Cultivating deeper understanding of identity, both one's own and that of another, involves a process of *cultural humility*, defined as a "lifelong process of self-reflection, self-critique, continual assessment of power imbalances, and the development of mutually respectful relationships and partnerships" (Gallardo, 2014, 3). According to Hook et al. (2013), clinicians must meet several goals to develop a strong therapeutic relationship: they must shift from a self-focused to an "other-focused" stance, overcome the natural tendency to view their cultural identity as superior, and be open to the diverse characteristics of the client in front of them. Culturally humble therapists embody an openness that is not dictated by their prior experiences and work collaboratively with their clients to best understand the client's unique intersection of identities (Hook et al., 2013). This humble way of being encourages a constant growth process that allows the clinician to engage in awareness regarding the limitations of their knowledge base surrounding client cultural background. This awareness then serves as motivation to align themselves with the unique background and experience that embodies the diverse client (Hook et al., 2013).

In the case of Marco, cultural humility might entail fostering a relationship with the family to learn more about their cultural practices and to discuss potential ramifications for injurious behavior. It may also be helpful for the clinician to engage in independent training to build cultural competence in working with diverse populations. Creating a relationship with the family might enable more effective interventions and allow the clinician to incorporate the family's cultural practices into treatment.

Critical Race Psychology

All of the aforementioned models and constructs point to a pressing need to consider the obvious influence of race in our all of our professional efforts. Critical race psychology (CRP) evolved from critical race theory (CRT). CRT was developed "out of frustration among scholars from historically oppressed racial minority groups regarding an inattention to racial power in critical theory and critical legal studies" (Salter & Adams, 2013, 782). As per Salter and Adams (2013), CRT conceptualizes racial power as a social science phenomenon that needs to be analytically examined via the lens of psychological science. The conceptualization of CRT, along with its five core elements, led to the development of CRP.

The purpose of CRP is to "foreground identity consciousness and race (ism) as a primary category of analysis within critical psychologies" (Salter & Adams, 2013, 782). According to Salter and Adams (2013), the five core CRT elements that assist in the development of CRP analysis consist of the following:

- Highlighting the analysis of racism as a systemic force embedded in everyday society versus the standard approach of limiting the issue of racism to a situation or a few individuals.
- Illuminating the ideologies that reflect and reproduce racial dominance in a manner that advocates for an identity-conscious style of inquiry. This challenges the conventional scientific wisdom that reflects and promotes White American interests.
- Considering interest convergence, which involves action toward providing people, especially those of White identity privilege, with knowledge to "resist the systemic reproduction of racist realities" (787). According to this element, racial justice has historically aligned with the interests of White Americans; thus, an interest convergence must take place that is justly sound for reparative action.
- Holding that "White identity (and its cultural manifestations) is a profitable possession that brings benefits to the bearer" (787). In other words, the possession of privileged identities contributes to the reproduction of racial dominance.
- Calling upon the practice of counter-storytelling and an epistemological perspective of oppressed groups to reveal and contest racism that is embedded in structures of privilege in everyday society.

These scholars explain that "cultural-psychological products reflect domination of the extent that they take particular (White American) understandings and pass them off as natural facts or objective standards" (Salter & Adams, 2013, 788). In summary, CRP provides a deeper analysis of psychological science. In the cases of Amelia and Marco, both practitioners come from positions of privilege. It is unclear whether they acknowledged or understood the impact that this might have had on their interventions with the families. This power inequity, coupled with past histories of oppression, exposure to institutionalized racism, and ethnic-racial socialization might have further reduced the families' receptivity to specific treatment recommendations.

A Practitioner's Perspective

I can still remember one of my first individual clients as a new trainee: a young man with potential psychosis symptoms. He was part of a Latinx family with monolingual Spanish-speakers. A majority of the clinicians, teachers, and administrators attending the parent-teacher conference were White. The client's mother appeared disengaged during the meeting, with eyes focused on the tabletop. Prior to the meeting, I overheard teachers discussing whether this client was being neglected; his mother had not administered the medication prescribed by a White monolingual English-speaking psychiatrist. Instead, the mother had told school personnel that she planned to schedule an exorcism.

The confusion I experienced was profound, and I was uncertain what my role was. As a Masters level, brand-new trainee, I initially did not feel that I had any power to help the family or to change problematic dynamics. Yet as a White individual, my client's teachers viewed me as an ally and the mother as a barrier to treatment. My Spanish language skills were conversant, not fluent, but when I spoke to my client's mother in Spanish at the school meeting, her eyes locked on mine. She had many unanswered questions. Something shifted in the room when she began to speak: a recognition that the meeting needed conversation, not condescension. The feminist tenets discussed in this chapter, and further explicated in chapter 4, served as a foundation for the subsequent intervention: sharing power with the client's family by hearing their concerns, giving voice to their preferences for intervention, and leaving with tools for future interventions. The family did proceed with an exorcism, but also agreed to meet with a

Latinx, bilingual psychiatrist and to administer medication. The school agreed to provide effective interpretation at every meeting. The level of pathologization of the family's decisions was greatly reduced by identifying their positive intentions.—Rachel R. Singer

Closing Summary

In order to fully address issues of child maltreatment, it is imperative to recognize the context surrounding an individual, family, and community. The *Multicultural Guidelines* proposed by the American Psychological Association provide one framework for analysis. Along with those guidelines, utilizing a feminist lens allows for discussion of potential power differentials between families, healthcare providers, and larger social forces. Key factors that impact individual functioning include one's racial identity, level of acculturation, and ethnic-racial socialization. Incorporating these elements into discussions of and interventions for child maltreatment allows for more culturally sensitive interventions that may serve to protect the safety of individual children. The next chapter discusses major approaches for responding to child maltreatment with a focus on these multicultural core concepts.

3

Prevention of and Intervention in Child Maltreatment

> There can be no keener revelation
> of a society's soul than the way in
> which it treats its children.
> —Nelson Mandela

Effective prevention and treatment of child maltreatment necessitates an integrative approach that targets multiple aspects of the system (Bronfenbrenner, 1977; CDC, n.d.-g). A comprehensive intervention program addresses individual and environmental stressors that contribute to maladaptive functioning, while also building on existing resources. Returning to an ecosystemic framework, the chronosystem, or time, refers to events that occur at different points of an individual's life. In the case of child maltreatment, this may include interventions that prevent, limit, and effectively respond to an abusive situation. Consistent with a public health framework, the Centers for Disease Control and Prevention recommend utilizing the following three-tiered public health framework of prevention/intervention for health-related problems that targets different points in time (Anderson et al., 2019; CDC, n.d.-f):

1 Primary Prevention involves intervening "before health
   effects occur" (CDC, n.d-f, 1). In medical terms, this is the

equivalent of utilizing a vaccine to prevent a physical ailment from arising.

2 Secondary Prevention includes "screening to identify diseases in the earliest stages, before the onset of signs and symptoms" (CDC, n.d-f, 1). Interventions at this level identify potential populations at risk for developing particular medical or mental health pathology and aim to prevent problematic outcomes.

3 Tertiary Prevention encompasses "managing disease post diagnosis to slow or stop disease progression" (CDC, n.d-f, 1). This stage refers to cases in which the problem has already arisen and the healthcare provider addresses the repercussions of the diagnosis. An example from the medical field includes using chemotherapy to treat cancer.

This chapter explores interventions in child maltreatment at each of these stages that focus on empowerment and strengths-based tools with a special attention to multiculturalism and feminism. Recommendations also include interventions at the individual, family, community, and policy levels.

Primary Intervention: Preventing Maltreatment

Intervening early to prevent maltreatment not only limits ramifications for children's mental health and family stress, but also may be much more effective and less costly than later interventions that address secondary or tertiary prevention (Arruabarrena & de Paúl, 2012). Specific tools include building on protective factors, connecting with communities, identifying opportunities for empowerment, and providing effective training for professionals on multicultural competence (Arruabarrena & de Paúl, 2012). As noted by the American Psychological Association Working Group on Child Maltreatment Prevention in Community Health Centers (APA, 2009), primary prevention is particularly useful in the case of child maltreatment: "Analogous to other national public health strategies universally encouraged for all families—such as vaccines, car seats, and breastfeeding—primary prevention efforts such as those focusing on positive parenting practices can have a far-reaching impact on children, families, and communities, ultimately challenging normative patterns" (7).

Interventions at this level tend to focus on supporting parents and communities, but this section will also focus on systemic interventions.

Identifying and Bolstering Protective Factors

If practitioners start from a deficits-based perspective, they may heighten healthcare disparities for underserved populations, perpetuate harmful stereotypes about communities of color, and also miss opportunities to tap into existing community or family resources for help and information. Shifting to a strengths-based perspective may instead limit negativity and blame toward families in highly stressful situations (Goodman et al., 2004; Herrenkohl et al., 2015). Indeed, this perspective is inherently feminist in that those in positions of power (e.g., gatekeepers in the field of child maltreatment) recognize the inherent worth and value of all families, including those involved in the child welfare system. There are a wide range of family and community factors that buffer against potential harm and reduce the likelihood of child maltreatment.

Parent Training. Starting on the individual or family level, a systemic literature review conducted by Altafim and Linhares (2016) examined the impact of programs aimed at preventing child maltreatment by both reducing child behavioral problems and providing behavioral strategies to the parents themselves. Across a variety of studies conducted in developing countries, a vast majority (e.g., 90%) of preventative interventions resulted in reduced behavioral problems among children. Key elements of parent training programs included interventions that promoted healthy relationships between caregivers and children, increased parents' knowledge about child development, and taught parents effective interventions for behavior management (Altafim & Linhares, 2016; O'Neill et al., 2020). Of note, some of the interventions that resulted in improved behavior and decreased child maltreatment did not specifically include interventions aimed at violence. Rather, the focus on healthy relationships between caregivers and children was sufficient to result in improved outcomes. These findings mirror a meta-analysis conducted by Chen and Chan (2015) which found that interventions targeting parent skills reduced rates of child maltreatment. For more on parental interventions, see *secondary preventions* in chapter 5.

Heidari, Gissander, and Silovsky (2018) found that regardless of location (urban or rural), families who received connections to outside services and supports were almost twenty-one times more likely than those who did not receive these supports to complete a child abuse prevention program. A single intervention program may not be sufficient to create true lasting change. However, having an interpersonal support system may encourage families to follow through on treatment and maintain these changes. Indeed, this may help more when paired with specific therapeutic interventions, such as functional family therapy, that aim to help families continue using effective interventions long after the clinician's formal role has ended (Alexander & Parsons, 1982; Sexton & Turner, 2010.)

Relationships. Unsurprisingly, many of these factors center upon relationships, an ecosystemic focus on the *microsystem,* or *interpersonal dynamics* (Bronfenbrenner, 1977; CDC, n.d.-b). Social support is particularly important, both within family and social networks. Families that are isolated may have limited avenues for seeking support for stressors. Connections to adults who are not related to the family may further bolster family communication and parenting supports, and provide an opportunity for parents to consult with a positive "model" or mentor (Bailey et al., 2015; CDC, n.d.-b). This also increases stability and positive communication strategies within families. Indeed, the *Multicultural Guidelines* from the American Psychological Association note the connection in collectivist cultures between symptoms and stressors within the family (APA, 2017b). The recommendations from the CDC (n.d.-b) also highlight the importance of both fostering positive skills for parenting and ensuring adequate mental health support for parents (CDC, n.d.-b). Parenting often increases conflict within families in general, and external stressors amplify existing challenges. When the level of community supports is unknown, such as for Miguelina's family, it is often helpful for clinicians to inquire about community-based resources or supports (e.g., non-family connections, religious affiliation).

Financial Supports. Supporting families' concrete needs is an integral part of preventing violence within the home (CDC, n.d.-a). As noted by Fortson et al. (2016), financial stability is a key part of this support. Indeed, there is a clear link between financial hardship and the likelihood that a family will be investigated for child maltreatment (Lefebvre et al., 2017). These authors recommend modifying how Temporary Assistance for Needy Families (TANF) is distributed, enabling the Earned Income Tax Credit (EITC) to "help low income families increase their income while incentivizing work or offsetting the costs of child-rearing" (13), subsidizing childcare costs, and increasing support for housing mobility to help families move to safe and secure neighborhoods. Families also need access to a clear source of income or employment (CDC, n.d.-a).

Additional financial supports might include altering policy at the state, local, or company level to make workplace policies more conducive to positive family relationships. Specific recommendations include 1) ensuring that all workers receive a living wage that covers the cost of expenses, 2) providing paid leave for parental leave, sick leave, and vacations, and 3) ensuring that work schedules are consistent enough to ensure a base level of income while also maintaining flexibility (e.g., compressed work weeks, increasing flexibility for work location, and allowing alterations based on childcare coverage) (Fortson et al., 2016).

In Bashiir's case, his parents were both working multiple jobs that limited their ability to provide childcare coverage for Bashiir's younger siblings. It is clear that modifications to their schedule, or increased revenue that would allow them to either decrease parental working hours or increase resources to assist with childcare coverage would be beneficial for the family to enable Bashiir to attend school more regularly. Further, the neighborhood violence discussed in both the case of Bashiir and the case of Jaquann is highly likely to increase family stressors. Policies aimed at strengthening neighborhood and community resources increase family perceptions of safety, and further provide safe places for the families and children to go outside of their homes. Haas et al. (2018) found that families appreciated the presence of safe recreational spaces for children, such as libraries, community centers, computer rooms, and pools. Indeed, it's likely that parents of all of the children discussed in the cases in this book would benefit from not only the safe space for children, but also the potential parenting reprieve to reduce parental stressors (Haas et al., 2018).

Recommendations regarding financial stabilization and upward mobility are particularly salient in a post–COVID-19 environment. This global pandemic has caused unprecedented disruption to work and school schedules, but has particularly impacted communities of color (Golden, 2020). For example, living in more population dense areas, status as an essential worker who is not able to take time off, inequitable access to healthcare, the presence of pre-existing and chronic conditions, and higher levels of stress have likely contributed to much higher levels of both illness and death among Black individuals (Golden, 2020). Bolstering protective factors may limit some of the parental stressors that lead to maladaptive relational patterns. Increasing upward social mobility can reduce risk of both child abuse and neglect, particularly given the overlap between poverty and violence within families (Goodman et al., 2009; Lefebvre et al., 2017).

Systemic Interventions

> While professional individuals are often trained on the procedures related to ethics and legal mandates for reporting child maltreatment, it is also necessary to ensure that these interventions are embedded in a cultural context. As noted by the American Psychological Association's *Multicultural Guidelines*: "Psychological understandings of what constitutes childhood, adolescence, adulthood, and older adulthood are to some extent culturally constructed and context-dependent, where a particular behavior of a parent or of a child is considered normative in one context but considered maladaptive or pathological in another" (APA, 2017b, 27).

The many forces of oppression discussed in chapter 2 are also present within professionals treating and intervening on issues of child maltreatment. Indeed, it is well documented that Black and Native American children were more likely to be placed in foster care than their White counterparts (Miller & Esenstad, 2015). Trainings on culture, identity, and effective tools for anti-racism should be standard practice within the field of mental health, but also among law enforcement agents, judges, and lawyers who are tasked with intervening after a problematic behavior has been reported (Miller & Esenstad, 2015).

In the case of Jaquann, the guidance counselor commented "Oh, I'm surprised to hear from you; I thought you had dropped out." This statement represents a potential microaggression as well as potential implicit bias: an assumption that absences equate with delinquent behavior. It would be very helpful for his guidance counselor and staff at his school to engage in a level of reflexivity to analyze the origins of this assumption, increase awareness of potential biases, and foster understanding about potential ramifications for perpetuating negative stereotypes (Sue et al., 2007).

There are efforts across multiple states now to address the disparities in services for families of color related to child maltreatment. Miller and Esenstad (2015) outlined some of the key tools utilized by various communities, which included: 1) mandating oversight over the existing racial disparities on a legislative level; 2) integrating an agenda on racial equity into all child welfare agencies; 3) using multiple methods of data collection and analysis to study the impact of multicultural competence interventions; 4) providing adequate training for all individuals whose work addresses child maltreatment to ensure an understanding of the impact of race and racism on the populations they treat; 5) creating partnerships with community agencies; 6) working with tribal governments to ensure compliance with the Indian Child Welfare Act; and 7) actively engaging with the communities and families who frequently interact with the child welfare system. These interventions overlap with recommendations for professionals to foster awareness of their own biases (Sue & Sue, 2016), and feminist tools for engaging in ongoing self-examination (Goodman et al., 2004). For more on integration of feminist tools for intervention, please see chapter 4.

Secondary Intervention: Identifying and Supporting High Risk Families

Secondary interventions shift the focus from broader tools emphasized in primary prevention to more targeted strategies designed to support families at higher risk of potential child maltreatment. Note that there is some overlap between goals and recipients of interventions at the various stages of prevention. For example, both primary and secondary interventions aim to improve communication at the family or interpersonal level. Secondary interventions often aim to identify potential risk factors and subsequently provide tools that may promote healthy relationships within families (CDC, n.d.-e; CDC, n.d.-g). Identifying potential high-risk categories within families has proven effective in the prevention and efficacy of treatment interventions for child maltreatment (Vial et al., 2020). Here we address potential risk factors for child maltreatment at various ecosystemic levels and review intervention programs that aim to support higher risk families.

Protective and Risk Factors from a Systemic Perspective

Individual. As discussed in chapter 1, there are several factors related to children themselves that increase the likelihood of child maltreatment. Specifically, young children under the age of 4 and children with special needs may be at higher risk for child maltreatment (CDC, n.d.-a). Specifically, having a child with diagnoses such as chronic physical ailments, mental health concerns, or other differences in ability increase stress on the caregiver. This may lead to higher levels of maltreatment. For caregivers, factors that increase the likelihood of perpetrating child maltreatment include the parents' history of their own victimization, a family history of substance abuse or mental health concerns, specific parent factors (e.g., young age, low education, low socioeconomic status, single parent status), and having caregivers in the household who are non-biological, transient, or both (CDC, n.d.-a).

Family. Specific stressors within family systems also increase prevalence of child maltreatment. These risk factors include conflict within the family, intimate partner violence, the absence of parental supports, intergenerational trauma, poor relationships between caregivers and children, divorce or separation, and general sources of parental stress (CDC, n.d.-a; Kiser, 2008). As in the case of Miguelina, intimate partner violence may connect to instances of child maltreatment. Lowered resources and higher rates of stress may increase the rate of punitive parental responses. It should also be noted that no specific risk factor itself leads to problematic family interactions. Rather, a host of stressors may amplify problems (Vial et al., 2020).

Community. Specific neighborhood and community factors may also lead to potential risk for child maltreatment. The population density of the neighborhood may either be a risk factor or protective factor. In a study conducted by Haas et al. (2018), one participant noted potential benefits of dense neighborhoods. "When you livin' down the way in the projects, the walls are so thin. And people don't mind knockin' on your door [asking] 'Hey, is everything okay over there?' You know, versus livin' in a house, and neighbors don't wanna be so nosey" (173).

Additional community factors that increase the likelihood of child maltreatment include perception of neighborhood danger, high rates of poverty, community violence, high rates of unemployment, having few safe places for children to go, the presence of abandoned houses, and limited social support (CDC, n.d.-a; Haas et al., 2018). Identifying factors that increase family stressors and subsequently may increase the likelihood of child maltreatment is a key step to allocating resources and targeting intervention techniques.

Interventions

There are many interventions that aim to improve relationships within families and to shift them to more adaptive means of communication and discipline. The present section highlights several evidence-based interventions that may apply to a wide range of families and that either incorporate or mesh well with multicultural and feminist interventions. For an additional overview of interventions, see Altafim and Linhares (2016).

A Note on Cultural Adaptations. Interventions that are evidence-based are particularly recommended due to the strong research foundation for enhancing relationships, improving family communication, and reducing interfamilial conflict. When selecting an appropriate intervention, it is helpful to identify a program that is both evidence-based treatment (e.g., has a research foundation that identifies it as an effective approach) and evidence-based practice (e.g., "the integration of the best available research with clinical expertise in the context of patient characteristics, culture, and preferences" [APA & Presidential Task Force on Evidence-Based Practice, 2006]). Evidence-based practice incorporates both research and patient characteristics, culture, and values (APA & Presidential Task Force on Evidence-Based Practice, 2006). Parenting programs for ethnic minority families are most effective when they are culturally adapted to the population they are intended to support. Specific modifications may include surface level structural adaptations (e.g., modifying language) and deep level adaptations (e.g., modifying content for cultural norms) (Van Mourik et al. 2017).

PCIT. Parent-Child Interaction Therapy (PCIT) is an evidence-based treatment that can be used at the secondary and tertiary levels of prevention for child maltreatment. Although there are a number of other effective parent management training (PMT) models, the National Child Traumatic Stress Network (NCTSN) references PCIT as having the strongest evidence base for young children, including those who have experienced trauma (NCTSN, 2019). Other PMT models may be trauma informed but are not considered to have an evidence base for trauma specifically. For these reasons, this section will focus on PCIT rather than other PMT models. Originally designed to target behavioral concerns in children 2–7 years old (Eyberg, 1988), this treatment has been modified for use with children up to 12 years old to reduce and prevent recurrences of child maltreatment (Chaffin et al., 2004). The goals of PCIT are to strengthen the parent-child relationship, to increase desirable child behaviors while also decreasing problematic behaviors, and to decrease parent stress, primarily through the use of a positive discipline program (Funderburk & Eyberg, 2011). Interventions include live coaching of parent-child interactions through implementation of two phases, Child Directed Interaction (CDI) and Parent Directed Interaction (PDI). In CDI, parents learn to engage with their child using PRIDE skills: Praise, Reflective statements, Imitation, Descriptive statements, and Enjoyment of time together. The goal of this intervention is to help parents develop a warmer, more positive relationship with their child. In PDI, parents implement tools to support children in complying more consistently with parent directives and in decreasing problematic behaviors.

Due to the association between parental stress and child maltreatment (Maguire-Jack & Negash, 2016), PCIT can be used as a secondary prevention model by decreasing problematic child behaviors and increasing prosocial, adaptive behaviors before parent-child interactions have escalated to the point of abuse. As a tertiary treatment model, PCIT can be used to intervene once maltreatment has occurred, to prevent recurrences (Chaffin et al., 2004; Lanier et al., 2014). Lanier and colleagues examined factors associated with recurrences of child maltreatment in families with and without prior histories of child abuse and neglect. They found that PCIT was associated with children demonstrating fewer behavior concerns, and that parents reporting decreased parenting stress at the first assessment point. Despite these improvements, neither child problem behaviors nor parenting stress were associated with recurrences of child maltreatment one or more years later. Instead, it was found that parents who had experienced their own maltreatment as a child, who had previously enacted maltreatment against a child, or who had a previous substantiated report made to Child Welfare Services (CWS) were more likely to engage in further instances of child maltreatment. Low income was also associated with a later report of child maltreatment.

Although these results highlight the intergenerational transmission of child maltreatment and point to the notable stressors that are associated with having low income, racial disparities in reports to CWS and the role of racial stereotyping must also be considered. Families of color are more likely to be reported to Child Welfare Services for abuse, neglect, or both, and are more likely to have their child removed from their care (Child Welfare Information Gateway, 2016) relative to White families. Similarly, physical injuries in children are more likely to be attributed to abuse if the child is Black versus if they are White (Lane et al., 2002)

Institutional racism and discrimination are embedded and acknowledged in the child welfare system and can lead a neighbor, teacher, or therapist to interpret a mark on a Black or Brown child differently than they may a White child due to their own racial biases. For example, in the cases of Marco and Jaquann, school staff may have been less likely to conclude that abuse and neglect had occurred, respectively, and may have been more likely to consider context or other explanations, if they were encountering a White child. When a child has extended absences, such as Jaquann did following his experience of being robbed at gunpoint, there can be many explanations that warrant follow up. If Jaquann's counselor had contacted his mother and inquired as to reasons for his absences rather than reporting directly to CWS, she may have learned about his violent encounter and had the opportunity to offer resources that could treat his symptoms and increase his school engagement.

PCIT is found to enhance parent-child attachment by strengthening parenting practices and decreasing the frequency of child behavioral concerns. However, to determine what constitutes an "attachment," "strong parenting practices," and "behavioral problems," one must apply a cultural lens. In doing so, the differences in values and perceptions of child behavior among cultures are highlighted. For example, a study conducted in Norway (Bjørseth & Wichstrøm, 2016) found that although child behavior improved when parents participated in PCIT, child compliance to parental directives did not. The authors indicated that Norwegian culture places a high value on free will and independence. As such, parents may be less likely to perceive their child's noncompliance as indicative of poor behavior, and instead may appreciate and value their child demonstrating independent thought and reactions.

In recognizing the variations on attachment and interpretations of both parent and child behavior, PCIT has been modified to provide more culturally sound treatment for American Indians and Alaska Natives, Chinese families, and Mexican American families. Leineman and colleagues (2017) highlighted differences between collectivist and individualistic cultures in perceptions of praising children, indicating that praising children frequently was seen as unusual in collectivist societies. Instead, in American Indian and Alaska Native cultures, parents compared their children to the elders in the community and took into account the degree to which elders approved of a child's behavior. While this practice is not recommended in the original version of PCIT, implementing PCIT with American Indian and Alaska Native families in the unmodified format would prioritize and impose U.S. culture and exclude the values of these native families (BigFoot & Funderburk, 2011). BigFoot and Funderburk (2011) describe a format of PCIT that has been modified for use with American Indian and Alaska Native cultures, called Honoring Children—Making Relatives. In this treatment, traditional ways and values guide the implementation of the therapeutic techniques. For example, BigFoot and Funderburk (2011) described parenting efforts as collaborative, communal efforts that extend beyond a parent dyad into the extended family and community. Parenting values focused on raising children with positivity and imbuing children with respect for others. Discipline included "noninterference," which offers children choices as they learn to understand rules for behavior. Other cultural modifications include allowing longer silences, longer coding times to allow for a slower speech cadence, and varying definitions of praise and positive reinforcement to include linguistic differences, humor, name-giving, teasing, and ceremonies. In addition, allowing parents to tell stories and including a talking circle can allow Native families to communicate with other families. To provide this and other multiculturally competent versions of PCIT, it is recommended that extended family members be involved, which may include adopted relatives (NCTSN, 2008).

Another culture specific modification to PCIT can be found in Guiando a Niños Activos (Guiding Active Children), which is based on cultural values of Mexican American families (McCabe et al., 2005). In this program, cultural values are discussed prior to the onset of treatment to assess the degree to which treatment will be modified. Contact is made with extended family members in this pretreatment stage as a way to increase social support provided to the participating parent. Clinicians consult with parents regarding their previous experiences with mental health and to engage in problem solving regarding logistical barriers to treatment. As part of this process, families are offered unlimited phone contact and in-home visits. Modifications made during treatment itself include referring to the clinician as Teacher (*Maestro*) and the Child Directed Interaction/Relationship Enhancement Phase as Communication Exercises.

Functional Family Therapy. Similar to PCIT, Functional Family Therapy (FFT) targets the relationship between children and their caregivers to reduce problematic interactions and improve parent strategies. Improving family communication and reducing blame and negativity lie at the heart of FFT. This family therapy intervention was developed for use in families with high levels of interpersonal conflict (Alexander & Parsons, 1982; Alexander et al., 2013; Sexton & Turner, 2010). Treatment consists of three phases: 1) *motivation*, 2) *behavioral change*, and 3) *generalization*. In the motivation stage, clinicians build rapport with families by identifying and matching the family's style of communication, with the aim of reducing overall levels of negativity and blame and to create buy-in for treatment. This also includes an emphasis on a strengths-based perspective of identifying positive intentions behind a behavior. For example, in the case of Amelia, her mother may have been frustrated by Amelia's backtalk and perceived her language as being disrespectful. The *tapa boca* may have been an attempt to reassert parental authority to remind Amelia to adhere to the cultural value of *respeto*, or being respectful of elders (Calzada et al., 2010). However, this action may have had the unintended consequence of excessive physical harm.

Rather than adhering to maladaptive patterns of communication, Functional Family Therapy aims to give every family member an opportunity to express their positive intentions with more positive outcomes. For example, a clinician would validate Amelia's parents' frustration with her behavior and encourage her to verbalize their frustrations. Conversely, the clinician might talk to Amelia about her intended message (e.g., "I want to be treated like an adult" or "I want to be given more space") and help her identify ways of communicating this message in a way that her parents might actually hear and respond to in favor of her preferences. In the case of Miguelina, it may also help the family and clinician to focus on the potential intentions of each family member. In protecting Miguelina's brother, her parents may have been trying to keep the family together. Their dismissal of Miguelina's experience may have been the result of fear about how her words would impact the family system. Encouraging individual family members to discuss their own perspectives dovetails with the feminist principle of giving clients a voice to share their own experiences (Goodman et al., 2004). Turner et al. (2017) found that FFT is both an efficient and an effective treatment modality for reducing child maltreatment among families of color.

Child and Family Traumatic Stress Intervention (CFTSI). CFTSI is another secondary prevention approach that includes a focus on family communication. This treatment was designed for use with children ages seven through eighteen and their caregivers within thirty days of the occurrence or disclosure of a variety of potentially traumatic events (PTE) (Marans et al., 2012). The aims of CFTSI are to increase family discussions of trauma symptoms, feelings, and coping, while also providing children and caregivers with coping tools to effectively manage posttraumatic stress responses. The goal of these interventions is to prevent the development of Posttraumatic Stress Disorder (PTSD). CFTSI includes individual, caregiver, and conjoint sessions. Trauma symptoms are assessed and discrepancies between child and caregiver reports are discussed, with the goals of increasing understanding of and communication around the child's experiences. Sleep hygiene and relaxation strategies are also taught to children and caregivers to facilitate coping with their respective trauma reactions and to increase the caregivers' support of the child. Case management is also a large focus of CFTSI, as non-trauma related stressors often impact a family's ability to access and engage in treatment. By providing support with aspects of care management, the clinician or case manager reduces stress and burden on the family that can interfere with treatment engagement and support of the child. CFTSI has been found to be effective with families of several different racial and ethnic backgrounds, including Latinx families from Puerto Rico, Mexico, and

Central and South America with a range of acculturation levels, Black families, White families, and those with a range of income levels.

Additional Parent Tools for Behavior Management. Programs that target parent tools and strategies have also proven effective in reducing conflict and maltreatment within families (Chen & Chan, 2015). Altafim and Linhares (2016) have highlighted other programs that may help reduce conflict in families through improving parent strategies and decreasing behavioral outbursts. For example, the 123 Magic intervention program aims to "teach positive parenting strategies and techniques to stop unacceptable behavior, encourage positive behavior in children, and establish a harmonious environment" (Altafim & Linhares, 2016, 30). Many programs aim to increase parental knowledge, such as the Incredible Years and RETHINK. Other programs highlight specific tools related to safe and effective strategies for discipline, including the ACT Raising Safe Kids, Strengthening Families, and Mission C. Many of these programs also focus on improving family relationships, such as the Triple P Program. Some interventions, such as the African Migrant intervention program, are designed with immigrant communities in mind. This latter program includes eight parenting skills development sessions, focusing on learning psychoeducation about child development, increasing children's levels of confidence, enhancing family communication and relationships, addressing finances and legal issues that impact migrant families, reducing family stress, and addressing different levels of acculturation between generations (Renzaho & Vignjevic, 2011). For more specific descriptions of each program, please see Altafim and Linhares (2016).

Tertiary Intervention: Repairing Ruptures and Treating Trauma

Although the secondary prevention programs described above are effective in reducing exposure to child maltreatment in populations that are already at risk, there remain a large number of children who will require tertiary efforts. Approximately one in four children will experience a traumatic event before the age of 16, with child maltreatment being one of these traumatic events (NCTSN, 2012) When children experience child maltreatment, they are prone to acute distress that is manifested in posttraumatic stress, anxiety, depression, behavioral problems, and social difficulties, among others (Cohen & Cozza, 2013; National Scientific Council on the Developing Child, 2020). If these symptoms go untreated, they can become predictors of problematic adjustment as adults. However, a number of evidence-based treatments have been developed that are effective in reducing symptomatology and improving outcomes for children exposed to maltreatment.

Systemic Change

In order to bridge the divide among individual, family, and systemic changes, programs should integrate knowledge of the unique strengths and stressors for specific communities while simultaneously acknowledging racial trauma. This approach acknowledges the nuanced nature of child welfare efforts and ensures an optimal approach for preventing and addressing child maltreatment and promoting wellbeing. Two such interventions include the Radical Healing Framework and the HEART Framework.

Radical Healing Framework. Recognizing the deep intergenerational trauma induced by centuries of oppression, French et al. (2020) discuss a community framework for healing. This intervention draws from a multitude of previous frameworks, including liberation psychology, critical theory, theory of intersectionality, and social justice education. This approach is geared towards Black, Indigenous, and People of Color (BIPOC), recognizing the impact of mass incarceration, systemic oppression, and subsequent racial trauma. The authors suggest that in order to promote reparative healing, interventions must include several key components, including a focus on resilience, emotional and social support, radical hope, cultural authenticity and self-knowledge, and critical consciousness (French et al., 2020). Critical consciousness refers to an awareness of the larger sociopolitical environment. In order to achieve these goals, the authors suggest that responding to symptoms or individual crises is not sufficient. Rather, clinicians should become agents of social justice, engaging in active advocacy. This sentiment is also echoed in feminist interventions (Goodman et al., 2004) and discussed further in chapter 4.

Healing Ethno and Racial Trauma (HEART) Framework. This intervention acknowledges the effects of racial and ethnic trauma on communities, families, and individuals (Chavez-Dueñas et al., 2019). The HEART program is based on the premise that healing requires identifying sources of internal trauma and external oppression. In order to elicit internal, individual healing, clinicians must also address the impacts of racism, nativism, and systemic oppression. This program also includes great emphasis on a strengths-based approach. Four phases of intervention include: 1) establishing safe spaces for individuals who have experienced ethno-racial trauma, 2) increasing client awareness of the impact of oppression on individual and family functioning, 3) strengthening connections within families and to community resources, and 4) psychological liberation through collective action (Chavez-Dueñas et al., 2019).

Individual Interventions

Trauma-Focused Cognitive Behavioral Therapy (TF-CBT).
TF-CBT is an evidence-based treatment that was initially developed to treat children exposed to sexual abuse (Cohen et al., 2006) and is now known to be effective in response to a variety of traumas, including other forms of child maltreatment (Cohen & Cozza, 2013). TF-CBT is effective for ages three through eighteen and includes treatment components for children and a caregiver who has not enacted maltreatment against them. This treatment has been shown to be effective in a variety of formats and settings, including individual treatment with or without the presence of a non-abusive caregiver, group treatment, foster care, clinics, homes, inpatient hospital units, and refugee camps (NCTSN, 2012).

During TF-CBT, children and their caregivers receive psychoeducation about the trauma(s) they have experienced, are trained in relaxation and emotion regulation skills, learn strategies for managing unhelpful or inaccurate thoughts about their traumatic events, and practice ways to increase their personal safety (Cohen et al., 2006; Cohen & Cozza, 2012). When participating caregivers also learn these skills, they are better equipped to not only support their child, but also to manage their own posttraumatic stress responses. In an additional component for caregivers, behavior management skills are taught that are effective for supporting children exposed to trauma. There are also opportunities in TF-CBT for children to discuss their thoughts and feelings surrounding their traumatic events in the form of a trauma narrative. The final component of TF-CBT is conjoint parent-child sessions, in which children may share and discuss their narrative with their caregiver(s). In having a conversation about their traumatic experiences, the caregiver exhibits their comfort in hearing about and talking about these events and models effective, healthy coping for the child.

As the goals of TF-CBT include reduction of posttraumatic stress symptoms, it is important to consider how interpretations of and responses to trauma may differ by culture. It is crucial for a clinician implementing TF-CBT to conduct a culturally competent trauma assessment of symptoms, to take the subjective nature of trauma into account. If a clinician assumes that because a child has experienced neglect or abuse, that they will without doubt be traumatized, they are missing an important opportunity to learn about the child's personal response to their experience. Just as physical closeness, dress, and traditions vary by culture, so do subjective responses to an objective event. While acute distress in the immediate aftermath of a trauma is almost universal, many children do recover with time and without clinical interventions (Cohen & Cozza, 2013).

In the case of Bashiir, the therapist considered whether he had been neglected due to his absences from school and his caretaking responsibilities with his siblings. Even if the therapist or child welfare worker determined that these experiences fit a definition of neglect, it would be critical to assess his response to his experiences. Given Bashiir's feelings of responsibility to his siblings and his concern about their physical safety due to gang activity in the community, it seems more likely that he might have felt positively toward and perhaps proud of his caregiving and his absences from school, rather than traumatized by them. If a culturally competent trauma assessment was completed with Bashiir and did not produce elevated symptoms, neither TF-CBT nor another trauma treatment would be recommended for him.

TF-CBT was designed to incorporate the subjectivity of trauma responses and has been adapted for use with a variety of different cultural groups, including religious groups (Muslim, Orthodox Jewish, Jehovah's Witnesses), ethnically diverse families (Latinx, American Indian and Alaska Native, Black, and biracial [BigFoot & Schmidt, 2013; de Arellano et al., 2012; NCTSN, 2012]), and military families (Cohen & Cozza, 2013). Specifically, to modify TF-CBT for more culturally competent use with Latinx families, focus groups were held and the research literature on treatment with Latinx populations in general, and in the context of trauma exposure in particular, was reviewed. Culturally Modified TF-CBT (CM-TF-CBT) was then created based on the culturally relevant themes that emerged. These themes included the importance of including extended family members in treatment; understanding traditional gender roles and parenting practices; spirituality; and beliefs about sex and sexual activity (de Arellano et al., 2012). In their work, de Arellano and colleagues have acknowledged the negative connotations associated with the concept of machismo. However, they argued that this was an Anglicized perception that missed the positive aspects of a man's desire and responsibility to care for and protect his family. The developers of CM-TF-CBT received feedback that it would be helpful to provide Latinx families, particularly those who have recently immigrated, with more education regarding what therapy is, why it is helpful, and what trauma symptoms look like. This approach may in particular be very helpful in the case of Miguelina, as the clinician considers interweaving psychoeducation with trauma therapy interventions and culturally congruent therapy. The machismo cultural concept may also connect to Miguelina's father's role within the family and should be addressed.

As part of the process of destigmatizing posttraumatic stress and related treatment, a number of cultural values and practices were included in CM-TF-CBT. These values and practices include but are not limited to *familismo* (focus on close family connections), *personalismo* (emphasis on valuing and strengthening personal relationships), *respeto* (valuing boundaries and differences), *dichos* (proverbs or sayings that convey values and behavioral expectations), and *cuentos* (treatment modality that utilizes folklore and storytelling) (de Arellano et al., 2012). In CM-TF-CBT, clinicians assess the importance of these values and practices for each family and incorporate them accordingly throughout each component of treatment. For example, *cuentos* can be used to teach affect identification and cognitive coping, and *dichos* can be a part of psychoeducation and other components. As clinicians are teaching affect identification, it is helpful to consider traditional values such as machismo (how a man or boy should act; an emphasis on strength and responsibility) and *simpatia* (acting in a way that promotes social pleasantness), as there may be expectations regarding how or whether children express their emotions.

It is helpful here to remember the case of Amelia, who used profanity against her parents when asked to complete a household chore.

A clinician utilizing TF-CBT without the modifications might encourage Amelia to find a more constructive way to convey her displeasure with being asked to complete the chore. However, if the clinician considers the values of *simpatia*, *personalismo*, and *familismo*, they may be more helpful supporting Amelia in the affect identification module of CM-TF-CBT. It is possible that she may feel or may have been told that she should not convey her displeasure about the chore, even in a more respectful way, in order to maintain strong family relationships and smooth interactions with her parents. Building on feminist and multicultural approaches, Amelia's therapist might encourage her to openly discuss her narratives of the family conflict and support positive communication without superimposing the therapist's own value system on the intervention (APA, 2017a; Goodman et al., 2004).

Strengthening Family Coping Resources (SFCR). SFCR is a multifamily treatment that has some similar components to TF-CBT. In this fifteen-week treatment, immediate and extended family members of all ages are invited to participate. Families' coping skills are boosted through the use of routines, rituals and traditions (Kiser, 2008) that are tailored for acceptability and comfort within and between families. Given that families experiencing trauma are often also facing a variety of other simultaneous stressors, this treatment has the goal of decreasing posttraumatic stress symptoms while also increasing a family's sense of safety and stability. In addition, families learn strategies for regulating their emotions and behaviors and for enhancing their communication. As they might in a TF-CBT framework, families participating in SFCR also create a narrative; however, the narrative in SFCR focuses on the family's experience with trauma as a whole. SFCR has been adapted for use with Latinx families and is often used with under-resourced families (Kiser, 2008).

Alternatives for Families: A Cognitive Behavioral Therapy (AF-CBT). Whereas TF-CBT and SFCR are designed for use with children and their parents who have not been abusive, AF-CBT is a treatment that specifically addresses conflict between children and parents who have used physical coercion or abuse. AF-CBT is designed for use with children ages five to seventeen and has been used primarily in outpatient clinics and in-home settings. The treatment has been found to be effective in decreasing child internalizing and externalizing symptoms, increasing social competence, and decreasing parent-child conflict and parents' use of physical discipline (Kolko 1996a, 1996b; Kolko et al., 2011).

Child specific components of AF-CBT include psychoeducation about abuse and its effects, disclosure of abusive events, relaxation and cognitive coping skills, social skills training, and imaginal exposure and meaning-making related to the child's experiences with physical abuse. In the parent components of treatment, caregivers discuss relevant factors from their childhoods and family experiences, receive psychoeducation concerning the impact of physical abuse, discuss the child's disclosures of abuse and identify parental responsibility for the abuse, and learn skills regarding cognitive coping, emotion regulation, and behavioral management strategies that are effective without the use of physical discipline. Family components are also included, where the parents clarify their responsibility for the abuse and the families learn communication tools and problem-solving skills.

Although AF-CBT has not been formally adapted for use with specific racial or ethnic groups, cultural factors do have bearing on parent perceptions of discipline, caregiving, and family relationships. Similarly, cultural values and children's understanding of their role in the family and expectations for their behavior may impact their experiences of physical discipline. In the case of Amelia, her mother gave her a *tapa boca* for using profanity with them and refusing to complete a chore. It is possible that Amelia does not experience elevated problems or symptoms of posttraumatic stress if she has internalized the expectation that children consistently comply with parental instructions and that profanity is not acceptable. Alternatively, Amelia may in fact experience the aforementioned symptoms if there are large differences in acculturation between herself and her parents, such that she has developed values more consistent with the United States. In this instance, she may not feel that the *tapa boca* was warranted and may experience escalated emotional responses.

Best Practices for Interventions

Multiple interventions are needed to eradicate child maltreatment, ranging from prevention efforts to efforts to manage fallout from harmful interactions. These efforts must include an ecosystemic framework of intervention at multiple levels: individual, community, and systemic. Additionally, these interventions are intended to interweave feminist principles of empowerment, power sharing, and the increasing of access to available tools within families and communities (Goodman et al., 2004).

Initial Prevention: Primary Interventions

Empowerment Through Financial Stability. For the most part, families with more resources experience more stability, and poverty is linked to higher rates of intimate partner violence and conflict within families (Goodman et al., 2009). Providing this instrumental support reduces parental stressors, increases the tools they can access for help, and builds stability within communities. These interventions are more cost effective than interventions at later stages of maltreatment, and also lead to more comprehensive systemic changes. For low-income families, the loss of a job and subsequent financial instability may impact rates of both maltreatment and neglect (Pelton, 2015).

Effective Training to Reduce Bias. All clinicians and professionals who are working with underserved communities of color must recognize the potential ramifications of individual and systemic bias. Effectively combating these insidious obstacles to equality necessitates both individual reflexivity and systemic change. Trainings on antiracism, utilizing tools for empowerment, and shifting their outlook to a strengths-based focus allows professionals to support families without overly pathologizing them. For more on these recommendations, please see the chapter 4 discussion on integrating feminist interventions.

Identifying High Risk Families: Secondary Interventions

Reducing Blame and Identifying Noble Intentions. Functional Family Therapy helps high-conflict families shift from negative communication to recognizing each other's positive intentions. This intervention builds on existing strengths within families while also improving strategies for their interpersonal interactions.

Strengthening Parent-Child Relationships. Parent Child Interaction Therapy utilizes positive discipline to increase positive child behaviors and decrease problematic behaviors, while also decreasing parental stress. These changes within the relationship decrease the risk of physical maltreatment to the child.

Increasing Family Communication and Coping. Child and Family Traumatic Stress Intervention aims to reduce the likelihood of the child developing post-traumatic stress disorder (PTSD) by enhancing parent-child communication and use of coping tools in the immediate aftermath of a traumatic event.

Reparative Methods: Tertiary Interventions

Reducing Symptomatology with Coping Tools and Talking about the Trauma. Trauma-Focused Cognitive Behavioral Therapy decreases parent and child maladjustment following exposure to trauma by providing both the parent and the child with psychoeducation, relaxation skills, emotion identification training, cognitive coping tools, and opportunities to identify thoughts and feelings about the traumatic event. Parents also learn behavior management strategies.

Building Routines and Stabilizing Stressors. Strengthening Family Coping Resources utilizes routines and traditions and teaches communication and emotion regulation skills. By helping families manage co-occurring stressors, a sense of safety and stability is enhanced, which increases caregivers' abilities to support post-trauma family functioning.

Breaking the Cycle by Increasing Accountability and Coping. Alternatives for Families: A Cognitive Behavioral Therapy includes parent and child components, in which parents take responsibility for using physical discipline, for abusing the child, or both; families learn about the impact of abuse; and children and their caregivers learn emotional and behavioral regulation skills.

Each of these levels of prevention serves to reduce harm caused to children and their families by the occurrence of child maltreatment. While each intervention has its own merits and value, none can be maximally effective and far-reaching without considering the context of the family's culture. By utilizing evidence-based treatments that have been culturally modified to include a focus on cultural values and interpretations of family relationships and child behavior, clinicians can more adequately treat the whole child.

A Practitioner's Perspective

The most crowded therapy session I have every facilitated was also one of the most eye-opening. Bashiir's family, the client himself, and several elders from his community easily filled the waiting room of the small community mental health clinic where I was a predoctoral trainee. In the windowless therapy room, every chair was full, and many individuals found spots on the floor. I remember asking my supervisors about the protocol for inviting members of the community into the session: How did this impact confidentiality? What happened if we disagreed on clinical versus cultural recommendations? It was a truly pleasant surprise to see how comfortable the family seemed in the room, and how clearly the elders understood the challenges faced by this family. They had relevant knowledge I did not, and over the course of a long therapy session came up with multiple names of individuals who could assist this family with childcare.

I strongly support the notion that clinicians have many adaptable roles to play in the therapeutic setting. Knowing evidence-based treatments is truly not worth very much if the approach doesn't mesh with the family system, or if it contradicts healthy cultural norms. Clinicians can flow between professional roles—advisor, advocate, facilitator of indigenous healing, or change agent (Atkinson et al., 1993). Knowing which role to take depends upon clinicians' abilities to 1) recognize their resources and those of the community and family, 2) clarify the family's expectations for treatment, and 3) foster awareness of ethical mandates. While the community won't always literally be with the family in the therapy room, squashed between the radiator and a wall, we can still build on existing support networks to create more effective interventions for preventing and addressing child maltreatment. —Rachel R. Singer

Closing Summary

Comprehensive strategies for reducing child maltreatment must include a multifaceted approach targeting all levels of a system: individuals, families, communities, and society. Intervening earlier using primary prevention strategies may be the most effective method for protecting children, limiting family conflict, and reducing the need for more costly later interventions. Secondary intervention strategies include tools to help families prone to conflict to communicate more effectively and build more positive relationships. Tertiary strategies aim to mitigate the effects of maltreatment and serve to help repair relationships. At each of these levels, interweaving feminist and culturally sound methods serves to empower families while also ensuring more effective individual and systemic change. The next chapter examines these feminist and multicultural principles and considers their relevance and application to situations of child maltreatment.

4

Using Feminism and Multiculturalism to Address Child Maltreatment

> If we are to teach real peace in this world, and if we are to carry on a real war against war, we shall have to begin with the children.
> —Mahatma Gandhi

This chapter explores the intersection of multiculturalism and feminism as fundamental social justice tools key to the prevention and management of child maltreatment. Specifically, we have adapted Goodman et al.'s (2004) six key principles of social justice: 1) engaging in self-examination; 2) sharing power; 3) giving voice to the oppressed; 4) raising consciousness; 5) focusing on strengths, and 6) leaving clients with tools. These authors offered readers a framework for understanding and addressing child maltreatment with an emphasis on introspection, collaboration, strengths, and empowerment. Throughout the chapter, we make relevant connections between these concepts and the case studies.

Social Justice and Child Maltreatment

A commitment to social justice is prominent across all helping disciplines that address child maltreatment, including counseling, marriage and family therapy, social work, and psychology. Specifically, the National Association of Social Workers ([2017] 2021) highlighted social justice as a core value and principle of its ethical code, stating:

> Social workers pursue social change, particularly with and on behalf of vulnerable and oppressed individuals and groups of people. Social workers' social change efforts are focused primarily on issues of poverty, unemployment, discrimination, and other forms of social injustice. These activities seek to promote sensitivity to and knowledge about oppression and cultural and ethnic diversity. Social workers strive to ensure access to needed information, services, and resources; equality of opportunity; and meaningful participation in decision making for all people (Ethical Principles section).

Moreover, the NASW *Standards for Social Work Practice in Child Welfare* (2013) urged "social workers in child welfare to demonstrate the core value of social justice, the dignity and worth of the person, the importance of relationships, integrity, and competence. . . . Acceptance of these responsibilities guides and fosters competent social work practice in child welfare" (12).

Additionally, the American Counseling Association (ACA) stressed social justice as one of the core values that informs its ethical commitments to the discipline, promoting equity for its stakeholders across all of its professional endeavors and the elimination of oppression and injustice (ACA, 2014). Moreover, the American Association for Marriage and Family Therapy's (2015) ethical code also espouses a pledge to social justice. While not explicitly stated or framed as social justice, the code highlights core values around equity, diversity, and inclusion—key qualities that ensure social justice.

Finally, the American Psychological Association (APA) emphasized justice as one of its core principles, noting:

> Psychologists recognize that fairness and justice entitle all persons access to and benefit from the contributions of psychology and to equal quality in the processes, procedures, and services being

conducted by psychologists. Psychologists exercise reasonable judgment and take precautions to ensure that their potential biases, the boundaries of their competence, and the limitations of their expertise do not lead to or condone unjust practices (APA, 2017a).

In short, all of these ethical codes espouse a commitment to social justice. They all champion an approach that ensures that these professionals have the necessary knowledge, skills, and attitudes to effectively address the needs of oppressed communities. Moreover, these aspirations and standards are clearly aligned with the tenets of multiculturalism and feminism, whose ultimate aim, amongst many, is social justice.

Tenets of Multiculturalism and Feminism: Considering Social Justice and Expanding the Child Maltreatment Framework

Given the focus of this book on integrating multicultural and feminist perspectives in the prevention and management of child maltreatment, the next few sections of this chapter consider the application of these principles in the child maltreatment arena with the aim of promoting social justice and potential ways to dismantle oppressive hierarchies against children, women, and communities of color. As Boyd-Franklin (2013) reminds us, we do not need to wait for larger systems to change from the top or by the orders of perceived authorities; we must be willing to empower ourselves as practitioners, researchers, educators and policy makers to take the necessary to steps to dismantle systems of oppression and foster liberation. As espoused by Dolores Huerta, a human rights activist, "Every moment is an organizing moment, every person a potential activist, every minute a chance to change the world." In the next five sections, we consider how the tenets of multiculturalism and feminism can inform our efforts, using Goodman et al.'s (2004) principles, as they relate to disenfranchised groups, such as children, women, and communities of color.

Principle 1: Ongoing Self-Examination

"You don't look Puerto Rican," was an expression Anthony heard often from others when they learned of his ethnic background. Confused by this sentiment, he would playfully reply, "I don't look like

Ricky Martin, Marc Anthony, or Jennifer Lopez?" Anthony would go to Puerto Rico every summer as a child to spend time with his grandfather. While there, he learned of the island's rich history and appreciated the diverse people, who came in so many shades of color. Less interested in their skin color, Anthony cherished the lively energy and altruistic nature of his Puerto Rican community. As he grew older, he became better acquainted with the stereotypes promulgated by the media about Puerto Ricans and he learned that the subtext of the "You don't look Puerto Rican" comment was a microaggression. Apparently, some people had internalized a stereotype of what a Puerto Rican was supposed to look like and needed to spend time dismantling this impression through ongoing self-examination out loud.

To this end, Goodman et al. (2004) observe that multiculturalism and feminism both recognize that larger social forces shape our identities as professionals. As discussed in chapter 2, human development occurs in a number of settings, involving the micro, meso, exo and macro levels (Bronfenbrenner, 1977). Consequently, as professionals, we need to understand how these forces inform our worldviews and our child maltreatment efforts in the clinical, research, and training arenas.

This principle of ongoing self-examination reminds us of the well-known airplane metaphor—"put your own mask on first"—reminding passengers to put their oxygen masks on first in the event of low cabin pressure before they help other passengers. Similarly, when working with diverse clients and families, relevant professionals need to engage in steps toward raising their own cultural consciousness first (French et al., 2020), defined as "the process of developing awareness of culture in the self, which can result in expanding understandings of culture and developing deeper cultural knowledge about other individuals and contexts" (Paez & Albert, 2012, 510). To this end, there are several frameworks available to help practitioners explore and understand their own particular socio-cultural profiles.

For example, Fuentes and Adamés's (2011) Socio-Cultural Profile exercise helps individuals examine various aspects of their identity (e.g., race, ethnicity, class). The exercise's aim is to illustrate how identity is multidimensional and fluid; defined by context; and associated with various levels of power, privilege, or oppression. Similarly, Hay's (2016) model, which is based on the acronym ADDRESSING, urges individuals to consider how these key factors inform their identities and socio-cultural positions: age and generational influences; developmental and acquired disabilities; religion and spiritual orientation; ethnicity; socioeconomic status; sexual orientation; indigenous heritage; national origin; and gender. As noted in chapter 2, intersectionality is a key concept related to both multiculturalism and feminism, and noting how each of one's own identity factors intersects with the others is important to gaining a holistic picture of one's own positioning. These tools can help individuals explore and consider how various aspects of their identity intersect to enhance, compromise, or neutralize self-based power, privilege, or oppression.

In preparing therapists to work with Black families, Boyd-Franklin (2013) discussed how she encouraged clinicians to consider their own cultural backgrounds and the potential countertransference that may emerge in treatment. She highlighted the genogram as a powerful tool for clinicians to engage in self-exploration. Similarly, focusing on Latinx families, Falicov ([2013] 2014) offered three training tools, the Ecological Niche Exercise, the MECAMaps, and the MECAGenograms, to assist practitioners in engaging in deep self-reflection. She encouraged trainees to do these exercises on themselves before using them with clients to better understand their own socio-cultural positions.

Implicit Bias. Another aspect of an ongoing self-examination process involves understanding our biases, especially as they relate to ethnic minorities, children, and women. Banaji and Greenwald (2016) address this topic extensively in their book, *Blind Spot*, which focuses on our hidden biases. The authors asserted that hidden or implicit biases reveal our preferences for certain individuals over others across a number of identity variables, including race, ethnic backgrounds, gender and age. Research on implicit biases reveals key characteristics, including that these biases are readily available; we all have them; they may not necessarily adhere to what we explicitly believe; and they have real-life consequences, leading to discrimination and disparities in the management of child maltreatment (Staats, 2015). The good news is that our biases can be uncovered and possibly unlearned. However, this involves ongoing effort. While bringing awareness to our biases is a necessary first step, it is not enough (Banaji & Greenwald, 2016). In their book, Banaji and Greenwald provide numerous strategies for minimizing the impact of our biases in our work with clients, families and communities. These strategies include stereotype replacement, counter-stereotypic imaging, individuation, perspective taking, and contact with individuals who are different from us (Devine et al., 2012). Many of these strategies are interrelated, meaning that they inform each other, and they become more effective with ongoing use (Forscher et al., 2017). As noted in chapter1, child welfare disparities exist in specific racial and ethnic groups and are fueled by racial biases (Child Welfare Information Gateway, 2016). One way to prevent and address child maltreatment is to assess, monitor, and address our biases.

Training. Given the proactive stance of this book, prioritizing prevention, we encourage academic programs that aim to serve individuals, families, and communities associated with child maltreatment to provide training that centers equity, diversity, and inclusion. This practice, embraced across disciplines throughout the country, could lead to better-trained professionals. Borrowing from the work of Fuentes et al. (2020), these important efforts can start as early as in the course syllabus. These feminist scholars encourage instructors to adopt pedagogies that promote equity and provide numerous considerations for the syllabus to help center equity, diversity, and inclusion. These considerations require educators to: engage in reflexivity; adopt a diversity-centered approach throughout the syllabus; highlight diversity in the course description and acknowledge intersectionality; develop diversity-centered learning objectives; decolonize the syllabus; foster a family-friendly syllabus; and establish ground rules for communication.

Additionally, French et al. (2020) offer a transformative model to promote radical healing within communities of color from the pernicious effects of oppression promulgated by White supremacy. The model promotes embracing collectivism; raising critical consciousness; promoting radical hope; fostering strength and resistance; and nurturing cultural authenticity and self-knowledge. These scholars provide exceptional direction around how to use these anchors to guide the training of professionals.

Cultural Humility. With this principle, it is vital to keep in mind that this kind of training and outlook is ongoing. As promoted by multicultural scholars (APA, 2017b; Gallardo, 2014; La Roche & Maxie,

2003), when working with diverse clients one must recognize that there is no end associated with cultural competence. To be truly culturally competent, practitioners must recognize that their efforts in this area must be constant. Essentially, cultural humility involves a "lifelong process of self-reflection, self-critique, continual assessment of power imbalances, and the development of mutually respectful relationships and partnerships" (Gallardo, 2014, 3). In her inspiring documentary, Chavez (2012) highlights key principles associated with cultural humility including engaging in lifelong learning and self-reflection; recognizing and changing power imbalances; and ensuring institutional accountability.

Case Discussion. When considering all of our case studies, readers will note that all the cases represent various cultural groups (e.g., African American, Latinx). When applying the principle of cultural humility, we need to consider our relationship to the following: our understandings of these groups; their intersecting identities; what implicit and explicit biases we might hold toward them; and how all these impressions might affect our work with clients and families in those groups, especially since research has found that "professionals who believe the court system is fair and rational will not be vigilant in seeking out checks and balances to racial bias and may also be less likely to seek training or consciousness-raising experiences to address their own bias" (Harris & Hacket, 2008, 199).

In all of our cases, there are opportunities to consider these suggestions and aptly apply this principle. For example, in the case of Bashiir, professionals working with him need to assess their understanding of Somalian culture, identify ways to broaden that understanding, if needed, and then consider how this information relates to the actual family they are working with. In the case of Marco, professionals working with him need to explore, among other things, how their religious or spiritual beliefs align and conflict with Palo ideology. In the case of Miguelina, Dr. Ortiz took the necessary steps to dismantle any assumptions he had about their shared Latinx identities. While they shared Spanish-English bilingualism, bicultural backgrounds and related cultural values, there were also several salient differences, including class, ethnicity, and skin color. Through ongoing self-examination, Dr. Ortiz was able to provide an optimal treatment process that allowed

Miguelina to adequately address her pressing treatment concerns in a culturally congruent manner, while ensuring that his assumptions and biases were continuously monitored.

When we as professionals consider all of the cases highlighted in this book, we need to examine our values and how they inform, facilitate, or compromise our work with clients and families. For instance, if we feel judgment of or contempt for the clients or families in any of these cases, is it because we are imposing our own values on these families? Engaging in ongoing self-examination is a key step to effectively preventing or addressing child maltreatment.

Principle 2: Sharing Power

"Anybody want to add anything to the agenda?" was how Professor Perez typically started most of his classes involving professionals who were committed to working with children and families. Realizing his own power as a faculty member and wanting to model sharing power, he would invite students to help co-create the agenda for each class session. Initially, students would remain quiet, not knowing how to participate. Typically, faculty came in and told them what was going to happen in a class, so they were slow to warm up to this approach, but through Professor Perez's patience, consistency, and commitment, the silence would eventually be replaced with an active agenda-building process. Professor Perez also opted to use pedagogical approaches that promoted active learning to illustrate collaboration and best practices for teaching and learning. For Professor Perez it was important to model for students how to share power with them with the hope that they would do the same with their clients and families, as they considered and addressed child maltreatments.

In this next principle, sharing power, Goodman et al. (2004) extract critical and overlapping components of multiculturalism and feminism that encourage practitioners and researchers to consider ways to share power with the clients they serve. Both frameworks are keenly aware of power differentials. They both recognize how professionals and clients can benefit and grow from the mutuality that exists between them, while at the same time taking steps not to abuse their power. Part of sharing power is recognizing that policy makers, researchers, and clinicians may not necessarily know what a family or community needs better than the stakeholders themselves. Hence, it may be more helpful to use a framework in which the family's or community's valuable insights are solicited and considered in interventions, policies, or research studies.

This principle of sharing power aligns closely with the spirit of motivational interviewing (MI), a well-established approach for understanding and facilitating change. The architects of this model, Miller and Rollnick (2012), defined MI as:

> A collaborative, goal-oriented style of communication with particular attention to the language of change. It is designed to strengthen personal motivation for and commitment to a specific goal by eliciting and exploring the person's own reasons for change within an atmosphere of acceptance and compassion (29).

MI emphasizes collaborative conversation styles strongly informed by the person-centered approach—an approach utilized by many helping disciplines. The major tenets associated with this approach involve recognizing people's right to self-determination. Specifically, person-centered care acknowledges individuals and families as collaborators and self-experts, who come with their own ideas, solutions, resources, and talents.

Often child maltreatment professionals come with the best of intentions to help. They may feel obligated to offer knowledge and skills related to the presenting concern. Miller and Rollnick (2013) caution against what they termed the "righting reflex," which is the tendency to want to "fix" problems, even with the client's best interests in mind. This well-intentioned reflex may compromise our efforts to share power and places our clients and families in a disadvantaged position where *we* are the authority. Instead, Miller and Rollnick (2012) promote an "Elicit-Provide-Elicit" strategy, which positions clients and families as partners in the process and acknowledges that the families have pertinent knowledge and internal resources to share. Once the clients share their ideas, the practitioners, with the client's permission, can offer their ideas (i.e., provide). A salient part of this step is asking for the client's permission to share ideas. The last part of this strategy, another elicit, invites the clients to respond to the suggestions, which again requests the client's perspectives, promoting the principle of shared power. In a family where discipline is the pressing concern, as in the case of Amelia, this strategy may facilitate a fruitful exchange that leverages the family's knowledge and skills, aligned with their values and worldviews.

LaRoche and Maxie (2003) offer an optimal prompt for facilitating the shared power stance with clients by stating:

> Please let me know if there are things that I say in our work together that do not fit with your values, beliefs, or life experiences. I would like for you to challenge me on these differences, because I think it will be useful in our working together (184).

While this prompt may yield positive outcomes and sentiments with some clients, practitioners need to consider the various levels of acculturation within families, as they apply this recommendation. For example, family members more acculturated to the United States might feel comfortable challenging a practitioner, while less acculturated individuals may feel uncomfortable due to particular cultural values and norms, as illustrated in the following case discussion.

Case Discussion. In the case of Amelia, it was evident that family members were in various places in terms of their own acculturation. The parents were more connected to their Venezuelan culture, while Amelia seemed more integrated, embracing aspects of her culture of origin and the U.S. culture (Schwartz et al., 2010). Hence, sharing power in this case may vary based on the family member and their positionality. Namely, the parents may assume a more deferential stance with the practitioner due to their reverence for "doctors," while Amelia, who is more bicultural, may be more at ease with providing feedback. This case illustrates how we need to cater to the unique needs of our clients, evading a one-size-fits-all approach.

Principle 3: Giving Voice

> "That phrase has always bothered me, because it seems patronizingly benevolent," said Cynthia, as she discussed the feminist perspective around "giving voice" with a colleague. "Oh poor [insert class of people], let me amplify your voice and take the personal/professional] credit for being so virtuous," she added.

"But it's still like, I have the microphone, let me hold it and turn it toward their mouth. The language that focuses on people who are 'voiceless' furthermore takes the focus off of the institutional and systemic processes that make those institutions and systems 'deaf'—not hearing diverse voices because the space hasn't been made for them in the room, at the table, etc." In this exchange, Cynthia highlights the nuances and challenges associated with the principle of giving voice (C. De Las Fuentes, personal communication with the first author, Fuentes, July 8, 2020)

In this principle of giving voice, Goodman et al. (2004) emphasize how multiculturalism and feminism both encourage the assessment, inclusion, and promotion of our clients' narratives. This principle encourages practitioners to consider ways to engage in advocacy on behalf of their clients. Herrenkohl et al. (2015) discuss the importance of changing systemic barriers to children's health through both community partnership and public policy. Including community members' voices in policy recommendations aligns with multicultural guidelines for "working alongside consumers, colleagues, and other mental health professionals to promote mental health concerns" (APA, 2017b, 61). Cheng et al. (2015) provide five useful and evidence-based strategies for assessing and addressing disparities in practice, including engaging in advocacy, that address the root causes of health disparities. They assert that disparities in healthcare, education, housing, and other arenas are associated with broader social and environmental conditions and stress that to be truly effective in helping clients and families, professionals must be willing to lend their voices through advocacy efforts.

Fortunately, many professional associations have facilitated these efforts through their advocacy arm. For example, the American Psychological Association developed APA Services, Inc. to help advocate for issues related to research, practice, education, and public interests. As seen in their 2020 advocacy priorities, APA engages in multiple efforts on behalf of its members and the people they treat, including in the realms of health equity, criminal justice, immigration, and discrimination (APA, 2020)—all areas that affect child maltreatment. Through APA's action alerts systems, within minutes, thousands of psychologists can communicate concerns to their congressional representatives and other government officials. In short, in addition to all of our good efforts in communities, offices, classrooms, and labs, we urge practitioners to explore ways to engage in ongoing advocacy through their professional associations and networks.

Additionally, rather than simply identifying the needs of families of color, Goodman et al. (2004) also urge us to give voice to historically oppressed or marginalized communities. Indeed, this charge dovetails nicely with the focus on empowerment in early prevention programs, or "the radical feminist movement that explains [child sexual assault] in the context of the imposition of male power" (Del Campo and Favero, 2020, 1). Effectively addressing these problematic dynamics involves creating partnerships with community groups and families to assess this population's needs (Nelson et al., 2001).

An essential component of any intervention program addressing child maltreatment involves the process of listening and responding to the experiences of individuals, families, and communities. Del Campo and Favero (2020) discuss the importance of both empowering and giving voice to the victims by enabling the children themselves to report their experiences of maltreatment. This may include large-scale interventions within the school system to provide psychoeducation to the students about what behaviors constitute abuse or maltreatment. Further amplifying the voices and perspectives of those populations most impacted by child maltreatment must also include elements of changing the larger structure that maintains these oppressive forces.

As discussed in chapter 1, ongoing, comprehensive, and strategic advocacy is key to eliminating child maltreatment and promoting children's right and optimal development. Gershoff and Bitensky (2007) offer four strategies to guide sound public policy in the United States to eliminate corporal punishment of children. The first strategy involves engaging in primary prevention efforts that offer a universal education program across the country. The aim here is to help shape the national conversation to one that prioritizes children's rights and development and discourages corporal punishment. The second strategy calls for more targeted interventions for parents and caregivers based on their particular needs and circumstances, for example, developing distinct programing for potential parents, new parents, and parent at risk for engaging in corporal punishment. The third strategy encourages comprehensive and sound training for professionals who work with children and families. Within this strategy, professionals who have frequent contact with parents, such as teachers, doctors, and clergy, can provide accurate information on effective discipline and discuss the harmful effects of corporal punishment. The fourth strategy engages in reforming local and federal laws that inadvertently or directly permit corporal punishment. The authors conclude their compelling recommendations by asserting, "as a result of their developing and vulnerable status, children should be afforded more, not less, protection under the laws and social policies of the United States" (261).

Microinterventions as a Form of Advocacy. Another way to address bias, discrimination, and structural oppression (e.g., microaggressions) is through microinterventions. As discussed in chapter 2, microaggressions are verbal, behavioral, or environmental messages that "communicate hostile, derogatory, or negative racial slights and insults towards people of color" (Sue et al., 2007, n.p.). Sue and colleagues (2021) developed a set of strategies for responding to microaggressions with the aim of disarming and dismantling individual and systemic racism and bias, which they termed microinterventions. These strategies also have utility when responding to the structural oppression associated with child maltreatment, which we illustrate here.

In the first strategy, these scholars advise us to make the "invisible visible". For example, if a statement is oppressive in nature, the target or an ally could simply inform the perpetrator that the statement was sexist, racist, or in the case of children, ageist. A statement like *"Children are still the only class we can legally strike in this country"* could help make this phenomenon more evident.

The next strategy advises us to disarm the microaggression. The main aims here are to stop the microaggression, get the perpetrator to reflect on their behavior, and express disapproval of the sentiment. In the case of child maltreatment, it often helps to remind others that children are people too to reduce the objectification and dehumanization of children. Moving children from property status to personhood can help with our efforts to reduce child maltreatment. Within this strategy it also important to validate the target of the microaggression. In our case, it could be the child, the family, or the community who experienced the oppression.

The third strategy involves educating the perpetrator. The main objective with this strategy is to broaden the person's consciousness and address their blind spots, especially as they relate to bias. One tactic within this strategy is ensuring that a person's actions align with their values and principles. For example, in the ACT Raising Safe Kids program discussed in chapter 3, parents participate in a "Box of Dreams" activity that solicits their wishes and goals for their children. In processing this activity, parent may recognize that their hurtful words and actions do not align with their dreams for their children, and this recognition could lead to reducing or ending harmful disciplinary practices.

In the last strategy, seeking outside support or authoritative help, Sue and colleagues (2021) recommend engaging in self-care, connecting with others to ensure their well-being, and communicating to the outside word that bigotry is not acceptable. In the last session of the ACT Raising Safe Kids program, parents reflect on what they have learned in the program so that they can become the protectors and advocates of children. They are asked to develop action plans for keeping children safe, healthy and strong. Sue and colleagues (2021) provide similar guidance on how to respond to macroaggressions, which include biased practices, programs, or policies that are embedded in social structures and contribute toward oppression. We list this book in the resources section of chapter 5.

Helping Clients Engage in Self-Advocacy. In addition to advocating for our clients, some practitioners encourage clients to engage in self-advocacy as part of the treatment process. For example, Alexander (2017) argues that "discussing self-advocacy skills and providing a space to discuss important social issues in treatment can empower clients to become advocates for themselves and their communities" (para. 10). This scholar noted that through this process clients not only gain personal power but develop relevant skills for addressing systems of oppression that directly affect them. This notion is discussed further below in principles five and six.

French et al. (2020) encourage clients to recognize the dialectic associated with structural oppression. On the one hand, clients need to give voice to this oppression and acknowledge the dark cruelty connected to it, while on the other hand, clients must imagine the potential for freedom, growth and wellness so as to not get consumed or paralyzed by structural oppression. They assert that this process is a political act that promotes radical healing, and we contend it is a form of self-advocacy as well.

Case Discussion. All of the cases discussed in this book would benefit greatly from the principle of giving voice. For example, in Jaquann's case, his absences were directly connected to the neighborhood's violence, which led to his PTSD. How useful would trauma-focused treatment be without addressing the root causes? In adopting the principle of giving voice, practitioners would need to explore ways to collaborate with local officials (e.g., the Mayor's office, city council, and local police) to address the micro and exo factors that are associated with this case.

Additionally, in the cases of Amelia and Bashiir, we need to reflect on how the anti-immigrant sentiments that have grown across the United States over the past few years have affected these families and to engage in advocacy efforts that will combat these ill-informed attitudes. One tragic example related to immigration was the heartbreaking separation of Latin American children from their parents as they arrived in the United States fleeing violence in their countries of origin. Thanks to the concerted advocacy efforts of many citizens, professionals, and activist groups, this practice was challenged in the courts and led to Executive Order No. 13,841 in June 2018, preventing further separations and leading to reunification efforts; yet, as of May 2021, 445 children remained separated from their parents (Kavi, 2021).

Finally, in the case of Miguelina, giving voice was salient to the treatment process, given all the oppressive forces in her household that permitted the sexual abuse and psychological maltreatment. As you may recall, misogynous attitudes were pervasive in her household, which led to Miguelina adopting a thin narrative around her gender, leading to inferiority. By calling attention to these pernicious forces, practitioners can lend their voices to dismantle these oppressive structures that lead to sexual exploitation and child maltreatment.

Principle 4: Consciousness Raising

"But spanking is part of our culture," said students in a training that Miguel was conducting with graduate students in Guatemala. While introducing the ACT Raising Safe Kids program, an international parenting program that prevents child maltreatment thought the promotion of positive parenting, some students shared with Miguel that physical punishment was a culturally congruent disciplinary strategy and given this, parents might reject the program if advised to suspend this practice. A lively discussion ensued, exploring the core cultural values of Guatemalans around parenting. Students shared how parenting was an important task to Guatemalan parents with the aim of promoting optimal development in their children. The students also discussed the extensive history of violence in the country and how political corruption created, maintained, and exacerbated this violence. They also started to realize how this history of violence started to contaminate and compromise their personal and familial values. Through these salient conversations, the students were able to tease out how larger macro factors influenced their micro contexts and related attitudes.

What happened to Miguel in Guatemala is aligned with the next principle, consciousness raising. This principle elucidates how for many oppressed communities the personal cannot be separated from the political, as it can be the very politics of the region that distresses, compromises, and destroys these communities. Goodman et al. (2004) acknowledged that multiculturalism and feminism both recognize the "person-in-context" conception—that systemic forces do shape our identities and overall functioning. La Roche and Maxie (2003) emphasize that our interactions with clients take place in a broader cultural context that will not only affect our clients' lives, but our interactions with our clients as well. In our child maltreatment efforts, we need to pause and reflect with our clients around national narratives and events. For example, while we may try to avoid politicized topics such as the brutal killing of Mr. George Floyd, we know that these types of national tragedies and the protests that follow affect our clients, families, and communities. In their Radical Healing framework, French et al. (2020) assert that critical consciousness, the process of understanding the etiology and impact of oppression, could facilitate the healing process and protect against the deleterious effects of racism. As proffered throughout this book, the child maltreatment arena is not immune to racism. Bernstein et al. (2020) reviewed the presence and influence of bias in child maltreatment cases. They recognized that "disparities in misdiagnosis of abuse may lead not only to unnecessary involvement of minority families in the child welfare and criminal justice systems but also to physicians missing actual cases of abuse experienced by White children" (35).

Through a narrative therapy approach, professionals can initiate conversations that explore, acknowledge, and foster the deconstruction of the cultural beliefs and practices that maintain and perpetuate the problem story (Goldenberg et al., 2017). Rather than adopting the "thin" or stigmatizing narratives imposed by oppressors, practitioners can operate out of a social construction framework that helps clients co-construct "thicker" or more accurate narratives that honor the complexity of their identities and lives (Goldenberg and Goldenberg, 2013). This approach can help clients understand the role of customs, laws, institutions, and language on their personal, familial, and communal narratives.

Case Discussion. The consciousness raising principle was used considerably in the case of Miguelina. Dr. Ortiz spent substantial time helping Miguelina deconstruct her thin narrative, as she had internalized the toxic notion that women were inferior to men. Through consciousness raising in treatment, Dr. Ortiz and Miguelina were able to tease out the variables that informed her trauma. Additionally, they were able to reconstruct an optimal self-narrative that highlighted her many individual and cultural strengths, allowing her to successfully finish treatment, graduate from high school, and start college. Much of this process involved focusing on strengths, the next principle proposed by Goodman et al. (2004) and other scholars (Chavez-Dueñas et al., 2019; French et al., 2020).

Principle 5: Focus on Strengths

O'Reilly (2020) reminds us of the power associated with words. In her essay on Systems Centered Language, she asserts, "language has been wielded for all sorts of oppressive purposes. Chief among them is its ability to frame worldviews, set definitions, and thus influence the treatment of people." She argued that in using words such as "at risk"; "vulnerable"; "historically"; "disproportionately"; and "more likely to," we are adopting deficit approaches with the referenced populations and perpetuating discrimination and oppression. Rather, O'Reilly suggests placing the onus on the systems that are responsible for the institutionalized oppression, advising us to "reclaim through language the inherent value of these humans and place accountability where it is due, which is squarely on the interlocking, intergenerational, and very present systems of tyranny and oppression, primarily racism" (O'Reilly, 2020, under the heading "System Centered Language [SCL]").

As highlighted by Goodman et al. (2004), focusing on strengths is salient to both feminism and multiculturalism. These frameworks encourage the use of tools to identify and leverage the strengths, talents, and resources of our clients. Additionally, helping clients reframe their persistence and resiliency during demanding times can help clients, families, and communities see their strengths, adaptability, and internal resources.

As noted in chapter 2, wellness and prevention efforts must adopt a strengths-based approach with the aim of promoting and enhancing resilience. One of the guidelines of the APA's (2017b) *Multicultural Guidelines: An Ecological Approach to Context, Identity, and Intersectionality* urges practitioners to "actively strive to take a strength-based approach when working with individuals, families, groups, communities, and organizations that seek to build resilience and decrease trauma within the sociocultural context" (5). In her work with Black families, Boyd-Franklin (2013) consistently found strengths in her clients. She observed families promoting an achievement orientation in their children, engaging in parenting practices that prioritized safety, and seeking solace and hope through spirituality. Falicov ([2013] 2014) also sought out strengths in her work with Latinx families, noting:

> Many immigrant families demonstrate capacity to survive and even thrive; they have ethnic and network resources, situational triumphs, loving capacities, and courage to face racial or ethnic prejudice and economic injustice. Strength-based explorations offer a more solid, hopeful ground for trust in the practitioner's capacity to appreciate and help a family (28).

Again, the motivational interviewing model, which appreciates the talents and internal strengths of clients, offers some useful insights to employ the principle of focusing on strengths. For example, Miller and Rollnick (2012) argue that practitioners should often ask clients about their positive attributes and offer back what they hear through reflective listening. They noticed in their work over the years that this strategy helps build a client's confidence and fosters hope. However, they also recognize that for some it might be difficult to identify strengths due to personal or cultural factors, so they offer a structured exercise called "Characteristics of Successful Changers." In this exercise, individuals review one hundred positive attributes and identify some that characterize or resonate for them. Once clients or families identify a few, practitioners can ask them to discuss how these attributes are characteristic of them. Additionally, Miller and Rollnick (2012) encourage practitioners to explore past successes with their clients. As noted earlier, children, women, and communities of color may internalize the hateful and oppressive rhetoric promulgated by the patriarchy. These exercises can help dismantle internalized oppression and expand the client's positive self-narrative.

Steele's (2011) book, *Whistling Vivaldi*, which focused on identity threat research, highlights the importance and power of a values affirmation exercise. Steele helps us realize that when an aspect of our identity is highlighted (e.g., race, ethnicity, gender), it may compromise our ability to optimally perform tasks. The values affirmation exercise involves individuals identifying values that matter to them and reflecting on the importance they give to those values. This simple and straightforward exercise affects people's sense of efficacy, interrupting potential cycles of failure and promoting successful future behavior. Helping our clients identify their strengths is key to feminist and multicultural approaches and helps undo the damage caused by oppressive forces.

Case Discussion. Our cases reveal the numerous strengths of each client and their families. For example, most of the families discussed belong to cultures that embrace a collectivistic orientation. In collectivism, unlike individualism, interpersonal connections, relationships, and group membership are prioritized and leveraged (Oyserman & Lee, 2008). This orientation promotes the inclusion of multiple perspectives, leading to creativity and innovation (Rodriguez, 2014). Additionally, through collectivism, individuals can secure much-needed support and comradery from the collective while facing oppressive forces and seeking radical healing (French et al., 2020).

Additionally, other strengths are evident across our cases. Specifically, Amelia's parents were dedicated to her well-being by ensuring she knows how to be cordial, while Jaquaan persisted with his interest in school despite the neighborhood violence. Marco's family was committed to maintaining their culture through their spiritual orientation; and Bashiir revealed impressive resilience in the face of relocation and had a power resource through his access to the community of elders.

Principle 6: Leaving Clients with Tools

"How are we going to say goodbye?" was a question Tameeka, a social worker, asked of herself concerning a family from whom she was about to terminate. The family initially came to the University's training clinic because son Mark (age fifteen) was having difficulties in school. Upon assessment, Tameeka realized that in addition to some concerning school practices, which she addressed through advocacy, there were some challenging family dynamics causing distress between the mother and her son. In helping the family understand their story, Tameeka realized that key figures, mainly father figures, often left Mark without saying goodbye. Utilizing many of the principles discussed earlier in this chapter, the family realized that they wanted to change this part of their narrative and have the option to say goodbye to people in their lives, including Tameeka.

Both feminism and multiculturalism involve efforts to promote self-determination and engage natural systems of support (Goodman et al., 2004). Given our emphasis on prevention and well-being, this principle permeates this book's overall thesis. The ultimate goals of child welfare programs are to reduce harm and promote familial health and safety (Child Welfare Information Gateway, n.d.). Hence, we must consider how we end our work with clients and leave them with promising and optimal trajectories. In short, professionals need to engage with clients, families, and communities "in such a way that his or her [their] presence becomes unnecessary for its continued growth and the empowerment of its members" (Goodman et al., 2004, 897).

Howes (2008) provides guidance around termination with clients and families. In addition to reviewing and recognizing progress, which aligns with the principle of focusing on strengths discussed earlier, Howes recommends considering what goals have not been met during treatment and what can be done to meet them. Howes also suggests developing a sound after-care plan to ensure the optimal functioning of the client and their family beyond treatment. In short, exploring and anticipating challenges can help clients, families, and communities plan for them, possibly preventing future maltreatment and allowing the family to reach their goals. The Association of Black Psychologists and their collaborators (Community Healing Network, 2016) offer a useful tool kit for promoting family, community, and self-care. This kit provides culturally informed tools for combatting anti-Black racism and promoting healing in communities of color in the face of over four hundred years of oppression.

Another tool we can offer our clients is a holistic perspective on their overall wellbeing, as we address child welfare matters. We write this book in the midst of the COVID-19 pandemic, which, as of August 9, 2021, has taken the lives of almost 204 million people across the world and over 633 thousand in the United States. Regretfully, the data reveals significant inequities. Specifically, the Centers for Disease Control and Prevention (CDC, n.d.-a) reported that communities of color are overrepresented in the nation's cases and deaths. They assert that "long-standing systemic health and social inequities have put many people from racial and ethnic minority groups at increased risk of getting sick and dying from COVID-19" (CDC, n.d.-d, para. 1). These inequities are associated with discrimination, healthcare access and utilization, occupation, education, income and wealth gaps, as well as housing (CDC, n.d.-d). As noted in chapter 1, COVID-19 has also affected the child maltreatment arena, placing children and women at higher risk for abuse and violence (World Health Organization, 2020).

As discussed throughout this book, practitioners must adopt an ecological approach as we conceptualize and address matters associated with child maltreatment. We suggest infusing the traditional biopsychosocial approach adopted by many helping professions (Henriques, 2015) with other models that embrace feminist and multicultural principles, such as Falicov's ([2013] 2014) Multidimensional Ecosystemic Comparative Approach (MECA) and French et al.'s (2020) Psychological Framework of Radical Healing in Communities of Color. These models consider key components that are salient to identifying and dismantling oppressive forces. For example, at the foundation of MECA is a deep appreciation for social justice and cultural diversity that considers factors such as migration and acculturation, ecological contexts, family organization, and family life cycle. Moreover, the Psychological Framework of Radical Healing for People of Color (French et al., 2020) extracts key elements of liberation psychology, Black psychology, ethnopolitical psychology, and intersectionality theory to guide clinical practice, research, training, and social justice advocacy. By broadening the lens, we can start to address the social and contextual determinants associated with child welfare matters.

By adopting a broad, multidimensional, and nuanced approach with our clients, we can start to not only address child welfare concerns, but also the social and contextual determinants that compromise their overall wellbeing. Take, for example, childhood obesity. As noted by the CDC (n.d.-c), childhood obesity is a pressing concern in our country with nearly 19 percent of all children between the ages of two and nineteen affected by obesity. Moreover, when compared to non-Hispanic White children (14.1%), Hispanic children (25.8%) and Non-Hispanic Black children (22%) have higher prevalence rates. A number of health concerns are linked to obesity, including heart disease, mental health concerns, and overall quality of life challenges (CDC, n.d.-e). The COVID-19 pandemic is a concern for the entire world, but it is more dangerous for individuals with underlying health concerns (CDC, n.d.-b) and regretfully, communities of color have been overly represented in this group.

In short, an approach to addressing child maltreatment that embraces the principles outlined in this chapter appreciates both the forest and the trees. In the wise words of Gloria E. Anzaldúa, a scholar of Chicana cultural theory, feminist theory, and queer theory, "At some point, on our way to a new consciousness, we will have to leave the opposite bank, the split between the two mortal combatants somehow healed so that we are on both shores at once and, at once, see through serpent and eagle eyes."

An additional tool we can offer our clients as we end our work with them is an open-door invitation. Given the healthy cultural suspicion (i.e., mistrust of institutions) and the stigma that exists in communities of color around social services (Boyd-Franklin, 2013), it is important to emphasize that their future involvement with social services may be warranted, but that there is no weakness or shame associated with needing to return. As Professor Perez, introduced earlier, says to his students, "just because the semester is coming to an end, it does not mean we have to come to an end." Just like cultural humility, our life's pursuits are ongoing and may require attention from time to time. Advising clients and families that you are a viable resource should they need you is a useful tool.

Finally, we suggest leaving clients with radical hope. Hope is trusting that change is possible (Miller & Rollnick, 2012). Radical hope "allows for a sense of agency to change things for the greater good— a belief that one can fight for justice and that the fight will not be futile" (French et al., 2020, 26). In order for clients, families, and communities to survive and thrive as they have for centuries, they must have radical hope. In the *Family Care, Community Care, and Self Care Tool Kit* referenced earlier (Community Healing Network, 2016), there is a section titled "Wisdom for the Journey Ahead," where Marcus Garvey, a Black philosopher and activist, is aptly quoted: "We have a beautiful history and we shall create another in the future that will astonish the world." This sentiment embodies the spirit of radical hope. In the next chapter, we provide a section titled "Final Impressions and Recommendations in the Case Studies," and discuss how we applied this principle of leaving clients with tools to all of our cases discussed throughout this book.

A Practitioner's Perspective

I was trained in a counseling psychology training program with an emphasis on multicultural and feminist relational interventions. As a result, integrating these tools into child maltreatment interventions seems essential, just, and imperative to me. Respect, so central in so many communities as a core cultural aspect of identity, is also necessary in clinical relationships. Clients are perceptive—they will pick up on values and judgement.

Conversely, "as the patient feels more accepted, and can let go of old expectations arising from experiences in past relationships, she can bring more and more of her whole person into the relationship with the therapist" (Miller & Stiver, 1997, 147). As a clinician, as an individual, and as a product of my own culture and identities, I also recognize that I bring my own value systems into the therapy room. Part of the challenge and the opportunity, in striving for multicultural humility, is acknowledging that families present in many different ways. In my family of origin, I was told that pursuing higher education was expected of me, and that being a student was my job. Furthermore, working was never a financial necessity while I was a student. I recognize that in the case of Bashiir, I initially expected his family to prioritize education above Bashiir's role as a caregiver for his siblings. However, collaborating with the family will serve them far better than a lecture about family roles and boundary setting. Understanding and acknowledging adaptive family norms means suspending judgment, or more accurately, engaging in deep self-reflection. When I do see my own values emerging, I must ensure that I don't inadvertently negate my clients' lived experience. — Rachel R. Singer

Closing Summary

The tenets of feminism and multiculturalism can and should inform our efforts to combat child maltreatment. As highlighted in this chapter and throughout this book, we believe professionals must question and dismantle patriarchal structures that oppress children, women, and communities of color in order to truly understand, prevent, and address child maltreatment. In the next chapter, we conclude this book with some closing remarks, offer final impressions on our case studies, discuss future directions in child maltreatment, and share relevant resources.

5

Conclusions, Recommendations, and Future Directions

> Children are one third of our
> population and all of our future.
> —Select Panel for the Promotion
> of Child Health, 1981

Child maltreatment is a major public health concern that impacts far too many young people, globally and in the United States. This book has focused on exploring factors that contribute to and protect children from this traumatic experience, particularly through feminist and multicultural frameworks. Incorporating a feminist view to our practices allows us to focus on the strengths of our clients, to analyze and address the power differentials between families and service providers, and to incorporate social justice tools that can contribute to the prevention and management of child maltreatment. These tools include an emphasis on personal introspection, collaboration, strengths, and empowerment (Goodman et al., 2004).

Implementation of these tools cannot be performed effectively without applying a multicultural lens. Cultures differ in their focus, and value various ways to parent and manage children, which is crucial to consider when attempting to prevent and respond to child maltreatment. Applying a purely Western perspective on these topics forgoes nuances in parenting and lacks respect for a diversity of values, experiences, and interpretations. Feminist and multicultural perspectives allow a richer and deeper understanding of factors that contribute to and protect children from maltreatment, as well as interventions used with communities and families.

Risk and Protective Factors Associated with Child Maltreatment

An examination of the literature suggests several individual, relational, community, and societal factors that elevate the risk associated with a child experiencing maltreatment. On the individual level, children who are younger than four, as well as children with disabilities, special needs or both, are the most vulnerable and the most at risk of experiencing maltreatment at the hands of a caregiver (CDC, n.d.-a). Considering relational factors suggests that caregivers with their own childhood history of abuse or neglect, or those who do not have foundational knowledge of child development or effective strategies for managing child behavior, are at higher risk of enacting abuse against a child. Similarly, caregivers who are socially isolated and do not have the support that is so crucial to raising children, those who experience high levels of parenting stress, and those who are themselves victims of violence within a relationship, are all more likely to engage in child maltreatment (CDC, n.d.-a).

With regard to community factors that contribute to risk of child maltreatment, the presence of violence within the broader community represents a potential factor that is related to higher rates of child maltreatment. Considering the fact that parenting stress contributes to the risk of enacting child maltreatment, it may be more likely that caregivers who experience housing instability and who live in under-resourced neighborhoods or those with high unemployment rates are more likely to engage in child maltreatment (CDC, n.d.-a; Haas et al., 2018). Societal contributors also include laws permitting the physical discipline of children and positive regard for this type of punishment.

The existing literature has largely focused on naming risk factors for child maltreatment and has provided a less in-depth examination of factors that may shield a child from these harmful experiences. Those protective factors that have been identified are familial in nature and require addressing the gaps in resources and access to basic necessities found between lower and higher income communities, such as adequate and consistent housing, health care services, and food and clothing. Relational factors can also be protective against child maltreatment, as caregivers who are stable, able to provide sufficient supervision, and who attend to children's emotional needs are less likely to perpetrate maltreatment.

Short- and Long-Term Effects of Child Maltreatment

There are a number of short- and long-term negative effects associated with child abuse and neglect. Children subjected to physical or emotional maltreatment, or both, almost universally experience immediate distress (National Scientific Council on the Developing Child, 2020). Although the impact of these abusive experiences varies based on a child's age, overall level of maturity, fulfillment of basic needs, and cultural background (National Scientific Council on the Developing Child, 2020), child maltreatment can negatively impact a child's development, social functioning, and psychological well-being. If a child does not receive treatment for these concerns, the symptoms can worsen and impact their broader functioning at school, at home, and with peers (APA, 2008). Furthermore, child maltreatment has been shown to impact brain development, including the amygdala and the hippocampus, regulation of cortisol levels, and functioning of the corpus collosum (National Scientific Council on the Developing Child, 2020; Silva, 2011).

A number of negative outcomes from the long-term effects of child maltreatment have been documented through the Adverse Childhood Experiences Study (ACES) (Felitti et al., 1998, 2019), which examined the impact of childhood traumas on adulthood functioning. These landmark studies found that exposure to childhood traumatic events, including emotional, physical, and sexual abuse, was associated with unhealthy adulthood behaviors, such as smoking and alcohol and substance use, mental health concerns, and acute medical concerns, including cancer and diseases of the heart, liver, and lungs, among others. In addition to the short- and long-term consequences of child maltreatment, death is another horrific potential outcome of abuse to children. Among those most likely to be killed as a result of abuse are boys, children under the age of three, and children who are Black (U.S. Department of Health & Human Services, 2021).

A Feminist Lens and Child Maltreatment

Feminist theory highlights the role of patriarchy in creating and maintaining the conditions under which sexism, sexual exploitation, and overall oppression unfortunately thrive (hooks, 2015). Although women have been identified as more likely to enact child maltreatment than men, excluding sexual abuse, a feminist lens highlights the role of a biased patriarchal system in contributing to this pattern. Given the sexual discrimination that is rampant in hiring practices and wages, such that women continue to be hired at lower rates and paid less than men (Brown & Patten, 2018; Jasko et al., 2020), women are more likely to be financially under-resourced and to experience elevated levels of stress. Higher parent stress levels have been associated with child maltreatment (Phillimore, 2018). While this does not justify perpetrating harm against a child, considering patriarchal factors that hinder women's financial and emotional well-being provides context for better understanding why women may be at higher risk of enacting child maltreatment.

Another way in which the patriarchal system may contribute to women being more likely to enact abuse than men refers to the imbalance in child caretaking responsibilities. With the general pattern being that women implement a larger percentage of the parenting duties than men, regardless of whether their work is inside or outside of the home, the larger percentage of women enacting abuse may be related to the proportion of time they spend with the children relative to the time spent by men. However, given that men spend a smaller percentage of time involved in childcare duties relative to women, the percentage of child abuse they enact suggests that men may be over-represented in the number of parents who engage in abuse towards their children. Perhaps male caregivers become frustrated when attempting to respond to child behavior, and if they are less familiar with tools that are effective for the child or if they have had less "practice" than their female counterparts, they may resort to physical tactics. Essentially, all are affected negatively by the existing state of affairs, requiring a disruption and a more optimal arrangement.

The impact of the patriarchal system spreads beyond women and permeates many other aspects of society, including the way children are treated. Historically, children were treated badly, abused, considered to be property, and stripped of basic human rights (Milne, 2013).

Over time, advancements in rights and protections for children have been made through efforts such as the Geneva Declaration on the Rights of the Child and the UN Convention on the Rights of the Child (UNICEF, n.d.-b), such that children are now seen as a protected group that is distinct from adults and in need of specific supports. However, the United States is the only member of the United Nations that has signed, but not ratified this Convention (Mehta, 2015). Application of a feminist lens would suggest that refusing to ratify a treaty that would provide crucial protections for its most vulnerable citizens is a result of the patriarchal system in the United States that prioritizes men, particularly White men, over other members of society.

Feminist Approach to Child Maltreatment and Mental Health

Child maltreatment cannot be adequately studied and understood without considering the patterns of systemic racism that have historically reinforced and maintained patterns of oppression. The broad reach of the patriarchal system extends to the ways that mental illnesses are conceptualized and diagnosed, particularly as they apply to women and people of color. Prior to the introduction of feminist theory, the field of psychology and its related research, theories, and practice were largely monopolized by men (Draganović, 2011). These male theories often pathologized and disempowered behaviors and reactions of women and people of color, as they did not fit with the patriarchal view of how these individuals should feel and act. Stemming from the need for a framework that acknowledges the genuine experience of women and people of color, feminist theory highlights the possibility that some of the behaviors and reactions that have been pathologized under a patriarchal lens could be understood as protective or adaptive when seen through a feminist filter. For example, a woman who dissociates during or after a sexual assault may be responding in a way that offers initial emotional protection from an even deeper pain (Brown, 2010). The same may be true for children who dissociate during child maltreatment.

Without taking feminist theory into account, mental health therapy misses an opportunity to fully examine gender and power dynamics, which can inadvertently reinforce the values of the dominant culture and perpetuate systemic oppression (Brown, 2018). Furthermore, if a clinician is not aware of and does not consider ways that systemic forms of oppression impact the day-to-day experience of the people they are treating, they are missing a key factor in conceptualizing individual, familial, and societal consequences of these racist and oppressive systems. They may not tune into ways that an individual may have internalized oppressive messages, which have been shown to lead to negative health outcomes (Gale et al., 2020; Moane, 2003).

Primary, Secondary, and Tertiary Prevention Approaches

To effectively prevent and treat child maltreatment and its associated impact on physical, social, and emotional functioning, an integrated, multi-tiered approach is recommended (CDC, n.d.-c). This approach consists of three levels—primary, secondary, and tertiary—that target different time points (Anderson et al., 2019; CDC, n.d.-c). These approaches give insight into various ways to prevent and intervene in public health concerns, including child maltreatment.

Primary Prevention

At the primary level, the focus is on prevention, which can include identifying and bolstering protective factors in caregivers and in the community. Supporting parents in developing positive skills for managing child behavior and providing access to effective mental health support are some of the ways that protective factors against the risk for child maltreatment can be bolstered (CDC, n.d.-a). Others include ensuring access to social and financial support, and making sure families can meet their basic, everyday needs (Lefebvre et al., 2017). This can be accomplished by making workplaces more family friendly, subsidizing childcare costs, and promoting policies that support working parents. Furthermore, making community connections, providing caregivers and community members opportunities for empowerment, and training clinicians and other professionals in multicultural competence (Arruabarrena & de Paúl, 2012) also constitute primary preventative efforts against child maltreatment. Larger, systemic interventions such as addressing racial bias in the child welfare system, tackling and dismantling systems of oppression, implementing work on anti-racism, and eliminating disparities in access to mental health care, should be advocated for and attempted by everyone when possible.

Secondary Prevention

The secondary level of this integrated approach identifies individuals who have experienced a public health concern, such as housing instability or job loss, and seeks to prevent the occurrence of symptomatology (CDC, n.d.-g, 1). Overlap can exist between interventions at the primary and secondary levels that may, for example, aim to reduce parental stress and improve family communication, which reduce the likelihood of child maltreatment. Secondary interventions seek to identify and support families who are at high risk of child maltreatment. Understanding the protective and risk factors at a systemic level, as well as at the individual and family level, would support communities and families in the goal of reducing the occurrence of abuse and neglect to children.

Clinical interventions such as Parent-Child Interaction Therapy (PCIT), Functional Family Therapy (FFT), and Child and Family Traumatic Stress Intervention (CFTSI) are other secondary prevention tactics created to equip parents with the tools to effectively respond to problematic child behavior, improve family communication patterns, and cope with potentially traumatic events. To work, each of these treatments must consider the cultural variations in what is considered "effective parenting," "problematic child behavior," or "positive communication patterns." Various cultures differ in their values and expectations regarding parenting and child behavior. Failing to apply a cultural lens to these constructs or treatment interventions prioritizes Western values and assumes a "one size fits all" approach to health and mental wellness, further disenfranchising oppressed communities.

The treatments mentioned here have either been modified for or found to be effective with several different cultures. PCIT is an evidence-based treatment that has been modified to provide culturally competent treatment for American Indians and Alaska Natives, Chinese American families, and Mexican American families. Honoring Children—Making Relatives is an adaptation of PCIT that is used with the American Indian and Alaska Natives cultures (BigFoot & Funderburk, 2011). Cultural values of Mexican American families provide the basis for Guiando a Niños Activos (Guiding Active Children), which is a culturally modified form of PCIT (McCabe et al., 2005).

Other culturally adapted treatments that can be applied at the secondary prevention level include FFT and CFTSI. Both of these interventions have been found to be effective at reducing the risk of child maltreatment in families of color (Turner et al., 2017). CFTSI has specifically been shown to effectively reduce child maltreatment risk in families in the Latinx community from Puerto Rico, Mexico, and Central and South America; Black families; and White families (Marans et al., 2012; NCTSN, 2012). Acculturation and income levels present other potential treatment factors that can be adequately addressed with these two interventions.

Tertiary Prevention

At the tertiary level of intervention, the problem (i.e., child maltreatment) has occurred, symptoms are occurring, and treatments focus on slowing and treating the progression of problematic outcomes (CDC, n.d.-g, 1). In this sense, tertiary interventions can be described as reparative and several are discussed in chapter 3. Trauma-Focused Cognitive Behavioral Therapy (TF-CBT) aims to reduce symptoms by teaching coping tools and supporting families in discussing the trauma. Parents learn behavior management strategies as well as ways to effectively support their child in managing symptoms of posttraumatic stress. Strengthening Family Coping Resources (SFCR) support families in creating structure through routines and stabilization of ongoing stressors. Communication and emotion regulation skills are also taught as part of this treatment. Finally, Alternatives for Families: A Cognitive Behavioral Therapy (AF-CBT) helps caregivers to increase their accountability for using physical discipline or for enacting abuse. Families also learn about the negative impact of child abuse and caregivers are taught emotional and behavioral coping techniques, all of which can help break the cycle of violence.

TF-CBT and SFCR have both been adapted for use with culturally diverse populations. Specifically, TF-CBT has been effectively used with various religious groups, including families who are Muslim, Orthodox Jewish, or Jehovah's Witnesses; ethnically diverse families, including Latinx, American Indian and Alaska Native, Black, and biracial families (BigFoot & Schmidt, 2013; de Arellano et al., 2012; NCTSN, 2012); and military families (Cohen & Cozza, 2013). A specific form of TF-CBT, Culturally Modified TF-CBT (CM-TF-CBT), has been adapted for use with Latinx families and incorporates values and beliefs that may be traditionally held in this community (de Arellano et al., 2013). SFCR has also been modified for use with Latinx families and is also effectively used with families who are underresourced (Kiser, 2008). While AF-CBT has not been specifically culturally modified, multiculturally competent clinicians will consider variations that occur in perceptions of parenting practices and family relationships.

Multiculturalism and Child Maltreatment

The literature on child maltreatment has demonstrated a negative impact on children's physical and psychological wellbeing in the short- (National Scientific Council on the Developing Child, 2020) and long-term (Felitti et al., 2019). However, people do not exist within a vacuum and the westernized ideas that characterize thinking within the United States do not fairly apply the concept of child maltreatment to all. Racism that pervades the United States also impacts the systems meant to support families in preventing or responding to child maltreatment. This can be seen in the fact that families of color are more often referred to child welfare services for abuse and neglect, and Black children are more frequently removed from their homes and spend time longer in foster care than White children do (Child Welfare Information Gateway, 2018).

Core Multicultural Concepts

To stop this pattern, a more nuanced and multiculturally competent assessment of, and response to, child maltreatment is required. To accomplish this, clinicians must consider a person's individual identity, which is complex and includes multiple facets such as racial identity, institutional racism, level of acculturation, degree of ethnic-racial socialization, experiences with microaggressions, and intersectionality. Examination and inclusion of these core multicultural concepts gives clinicians a more complete picture of their clients and the concerns they bring to therapy.

Racial Identity. Racial identity is a layer of individual identity that stems from a person's membership in a racial or ethnic group (Sue & Sue, 2016). Although awareness of racial identity has increased over time, Black and Brown people continue to face a multitude of inequities. Failure to recognize and address these inequities makes those who look the other way complicit in these injustices and invalidates the lived experience of so many people of color. This process of invalidation, often found in a colorblindness approach, further exacerbates the disparities and contributes to a biased and potentially unjust treatment system (Neville & Awad, 2014). In contrast to a colorblindness perspective, taking an approach that is color-conscious acknowledges the very real day-to-day experiences of microaggressions, racism, and institutional racism experienced by people of color and attempts to mitigate some of that harm. By recognizing an individual's racial identity and incorporating it into treatment and other interventions, clinicians gain insight into factors influencing that person's sense of worth and potential responses to situations and interventions. In the context of assessing and responding to child maltreatment, having a more nuanced understanding of the influence of racial identity is especially important, given that families of color may have an adaptive skepticism of health systems, law enforcement, or both, as these systems have been perpetrators of systemic racism and oppression.

Institutional Racism. Institutional racism refers to that which has permeated large, external systems such as healthcare, schools, the justice system, voting access, and the housing market (Jones, 2000). In each of these and other systems affected by institutional racism, people of color are denied equal access to rights, opportunities, and services due to unjust, discriminatory social and structural policies. Through the use of these discriminatory practices, forced acculturation of people of color can often occur (Sue & Sue, 2016), which then contributes to a negative impact on their mental and physical well-being (Saleem & Lambert, 2016).

For families of color, institutional racism in the child welfare system contributes to children's injuries being attributed more frequently to abuse, more frequent removal from their homes, and subsequently longer time spent in foster care relative to their White peers (Child Welfare Information Gateway, 2018). Furthermore, institutional racism has a negative bearing on the quality of schools, neighborhoods, caregivers' employment opportunities, and the quality of a family's home (Saleem & Lambert, 2016). Whereas owning a home can increase a family's access to equity, a more fully resourced school system, economic opportunities, and transportation (Szto, 2013), the policy of "redlining" has historically and persistently limited Black and Brown people's ability to purchase homes within desirable neighborhoods. Given the association between parental stress and child maltreatment (Phillimore, 2018), these discriminatory practices within institutional systems can be said to put children and families at higher risk of child maltreatment and intimate partner violence (Gibbs et al., 2017; Goodman et al., 2009).

Acculturation. Clinicians must also consider the cultural dynamics among the child, parents, and clinician. As noted in earlier chapters, acculturation refers to the degree of connection an individual maintains with the culture of both their country of origin and their country of residence. Individuals within the same family may have different levels of acculturation. Families that are more acculturated are more likely to understand or relate to westernized styles of thinking and, more specifically, a view of child behavior and maltreatment common in the United States. Relatedly, higher levels of acculturation may lead family members to be more comfortable asserting their opinions or challenging a clinician if they find themselves in therapy in general or in treatment addressing child maltreatment. However, it is also possible that clinicians could exhibit implicit negative biases towards families that are less acculturated.

Ethnic-Racial Socialization. Ethnic-racial socialization, or relaying information about race, culture, and ethnicity from caregivers to children (Hughes et al., 2006), is also related to individual identity. Through ethnic-racial socialization, children are educated on what it means to be a member of a particular racial or ethnic group. This education contributes to development and enhancement of ethnic and racial pride. Modeling and direct instruction are modes for passing down cultural traditions, beliefs, and history of a family's racial or ethnic group. Although ethnic-racial socialization can impart positive learning and pride, it also provides children with cautionary tales about racist stereotypes, discrimination, and ways to cope with these painful and likely chronic experiences (Hughes et al., 2006; White-Johnson et al. 2010). When ethnic-racial socialization is applied to child maltreatment, it can be seen that behaviors that may be classified as abusive in one scenario may be viewed as culturally normative in another (Raman & Hodes, 2012).

Microaggressions. Microaggressions are additional forms of harm that may heighten stress levels in families of color and may also impact their responses to potential interventions. Microaggressions are messages conveyed through verbal, behavioral, or environmental means that signal hostility, offensiveness, and insult to people of color (Sue et al., 2007). These messages may be intentional or unintentional, with many people expressing a lack of intent. Nevertheless, these insults create distress and harm in three forms: microassaults, microinsults, and microinvalidations (Sue et al., 2007). Microassaults are the most explicit and overtly racist. These are verbal or nonverbal insults or attacks that are intentional in imparting pain and discrimination. In contrast, microinsults are subtler in their racism and insensitivity to racial identity. For example, a clinician may not attempt to pronounce a client's name because it is not familiar to them, or a person may ask a colleague of color about their path to educational and workplace success, but not ask these questions of their White colleagues. Similarly, microinvalidations negate the experiences, thoughts, and feelings of people of color. An example can be found in someone who invalidates the feelings of a person of color by insisting that a transgression was not "meant that way."

DeAngelis (2009) points out the immense difficulty often associated with prompting White people to expand their awareness of these microaggressions from the academic to the personal. That may be because of the dissonance involved when people, particularly those who consider themselves to be "allies," recognize that they too harbor unconscious and implicit bias toward people of color and act in ways that can cause harm (DeAngelis, 2009). Mental health clinicians often enter the field because of a desire to help others. It can be difficult to then face the fact that not only do individual clinicians, but also policies and institutions involved in the helping professions, enact microaggressions that cause harm. However, it is far more detrimental to the clients we serve to pretend that these microaggressions do not exist, as they affect the ways we approach child maltreatment, and if microaggressions go unaddressed, they ensure that these negative cycles of harm persist.

Intersectionality. As clinicians apply a competent multicultural approach to assessment and intervention with culturally diverse families, they must consider the concept of intersectionality, which is related to both multiculturalism and feminism. Intersectionality focuses on the ways that various aspects of a person's identity intersect and contribute to a unique and often enhanced response to racism and oppression relative to a person from a single oppressed group (Howard & Renfrow, 2014). This aspect of individual identity is one that clinicians can better understand by following the APA's (2017b) *Multicultural Guidelines: An Ecological Approach to Context, Identity, and Intersectionality* and applying a strengths-based approach to their work with families. For example, looking for the strengths within a patient who is a Black mother gives that clinician a truer sense of the person's individual identity and informs the clinician's development of a more specific approach to treatment planning and intervention. Boyd-Franklin (2013) found that within Black families, children were encouraged to adopt an achievement orientation, parents prioritized safety practices, and families maintained a sense of hope and relief through spirituality, all of which are strengths that helped them cope with what could be very challenging circumstances.

Feminism as a Call to Action

Applying a feminist lens to cases involving child maltreatment contributes to a nuanced understanding of factors that contribute to its occurrence on individual and systemic levels. In addition, feminism calls one to act and outlines mechanisms for doing so. Specifically, Goodman and colleagues (2004) describe ways to examine oneself for biases and motives, share power with clients and others around us, amplify the voices of oppressed people, raise awareness and consciousness, focus on individual and community strengths, and provide useful and applicable tools to clients. Regarding self-examination, clinicians are most effective with their clients if they themselves consider their implicit biases, practice cultural humility, and engage in ongoing academic and therapeutic training in these domains. Furthermore, Cheng and colleagues (2015) suggest that this self-examination is a step towards advocacy work, in which clinicians identify and seek to eliminate disparities in health care.

These tools for action stem from and inspire a commitment to social justice. A common thread across the disciplines of counseling, marriage and family therapy, social work, and psychology is a high value placed on the ethical duty to practice social justice. It is not enough for clinicians and other service providers to notice and denounce biases within institutions designed to help and not oppress. We must heed the call to act, to stand up, to advocate, to make change. To do this in a way that does not impart more harm to already mistreated and oppressed peoples and communities, clinicians must be aware of their own personal and implicit biases. We must recognize the reality of White supremacy and work to do better as individuals, as mental health care providers, and as members of institutions. In the wake of a global pandemic that has disproportionately affected people and communities of color and in the continued systemic injustices and police brutality against men, women, and children of color, there has been an increased focus on making real and sustainable change. There is no simple answer to the need for change, particularly on the level that is required. Collective beginnings and steps forward, such as receiving in-depth training in programs related to diversity, equity, and inclusion, and promoting clients' self-determination and engagement with existing systems of support, can offer ways for mental health providers to contribute to the change.

Implications for Policy and Research

We can see many ways that policy and research can provide important steps towards preventing and addressing child maltreatment and answering feminist theory's call to action. Putting forth and supporting policy aimed at dismantling structural racism and providing more equitable access to education, housing, effective medical care, and justice has the potential for wide-reaching impact on child maltreatment (Molnar & Beardslee, 2014). For example, research on the relationships between communities and outcomes has shown that positive changes in the broader environment lead to community members feeling more empowered and having a sense of "collective efficacy." In turn, this has been associated with decreased levels of parental stress and child maltreatment (Molnar & Beardslee, 2014).

A striking example of child maltreatment can be seen in the Trump administration's policy of separating children from their families at the border. This cruel policy had horrific effects on thousands of youth and family members and was described by the American Psychological Association (2018) and the American Academy of Pediatrics (Oberg et al., 2021) as torture. The approval of the torture of children by the U.S. government provides an extreme and violent example of policy gone wrong. Instead of promoting child welfare, this policy stood firmly against that and instead promoted child maltreatment in the most profound way. Examining policy through the lens of child maltreatment suggests a multitude of ways that our society and government can do better. Legislation that targets immigration reform would reduce some of the traumatic aspects of the immigration journey, and as a result contribute to a reduction in government sanctioned child maltreatment.

There are countless other ways that policy has the potential to prevent and mitigate the effects of child maltreatment. At the time of the writing of this book, the United States had very recently moved into a new presidential administration and witnessed President Biden sign legislation phasing out for-profit prison contracts and acknowledge the government's role in implementing discriminatory housing policies (CBS News, 2021). As people of color are disproportionately incarcerated and adversely affected by racist housing policies, this legislation has the potential to inch our society forward in terms of providing more equitable access to justice, housing, and financial and familial welfare. Increasing equitable access to these and other basic human rights has the potential to strengthen our society, families of color, and as a result, benefit children. As we have seen parental stress to be a predictor of child maltreatment (Maguire-Jack & Negash, 2016), reducing these profound familial stressors can contribute to a reduction in child maltreatment.

The implications seen here for policy go hand in hand with implications for research. Studies have begun to show the hazardous effects of the Trump administration's immigration policies on youth. For example, Wray-Lake and colleagues (2018) found that Latinx youth felt marginalized and threatened by these immigration policies, and experienced anger and fear. Research on racial trauma highlights the harmful individual and collective impact of racism and discrimination (Comas-Diaz et al., 2019). Considering Wray-Lake and colleagues' (2018) findings, the youth they assessed were experiencing personal racial trauma and fear, and then re-experienced that trauma by witnessing the same events happening to others. As more research is completed on the outcomes of a policy that targeted family separation and detention of children, we are certain to learn even more about the harmful and profound effects that children and families experienced.

Research on child maltreatment in the context of racist policies and racial trauma can then be used to further inform policy development, intervention strategies, and prevention tools for child maltreatment. Furthermore, expanding this research beyond the individual experience to the experiences of communities will further respect cultural differences and strengths that can be incorporated into policies and interventions. By amplifying the voices and experiences of people of color, we have the ability to begin to do the long-awaited work of dismantling systemic racism and creating more equitable experiences, through which children and families can thrive.

Final Impressions and Recommendations in the Case Studies

The Case of Bashiir

Going back to the case of Bashiir, he was a sixteen-year-old male who immigrated to the United States with his parents and six siblings. He was responsible for caring for his siblings during the day, as his parents worked multiple jobs. Due to his absences from school, Bashiir was referred to therapy by school staff out of concern for potential neglect. Multiple variables should be considered when deciding both whether his absences constituted neglect and how best to support Bashiir and his family. The school took the perspective that Bashiir's family was out of compliance with the requirement for a child his age to attend school. While this may technically be accurate, this view omits the context of the family's experiences and misses several other key factors related to Bashiir's family and culture. Viewing the family's behavior as wrong or even harmful stems from a narrow perspective that "others" the family and implies that there is a "correct" way to behave (Hook et al., 2013). We recommend that the clinician exercise cultural humility (Gallardo, 2014), as this will broaden their perspective on various cultural values held by the family, and suggest a more expansive number of options to explain Bashiir's absences, none of which are "incorrect," but which stem from different, but valid, perspectives.

As the oldest child, Bashiir's familial and cultural values ascribe him responsibility for tending to his siblings. It could be said that Bashiir is being parentified and that this is impairing his functioning by impacting his school attendance. However, viewing him as parentified may be a westernized perspective, as the United States places a strong emphasis on individual, rather than collectivist needs and priorities. To provide a more inclusive conceptualization that takes Bashiir's cultural and familial values into account, his clinician should assess both Bashiir's and his family's level of comfort and distress with Bashiir's role as a caretaker for his siblings. If he or they do not wish for him to be in this role, but state that it is a matter of necessity, the clinician can work with the family to consider other options. Alternatively, Bashiir, his parents, or both may prefer and find value in his role as a caretaker. In either instance, the clinician should take the family's preferences and needs for support into account. In doing so, we recommend that the clinician consider the family's documentation status. If the family is not documented in the United States, they may have an adaptive and realistic fear of pursuing official means of support. The family may then be more comfortable seeking family or community supports to build a system in which Bashiir can care for his siblings, if preferred, and also attend school. Through a narrative therapy approach, the family could begin the process of authoring a narrative that is inclusive of all these nuances and factors. In this case, the clinician, following a culturally informed approach, was able work with the elders in the community to explore resources and secure support for the family, which led to the successful resolution of a number of the family's concerns.

The Case of Amelia

To revisit the case of Amelia, she was a fourteen-year-old Latinx female who immigrated to the United States with her family from Venezuela when she was ten years old. Amelia frequently served as the family's interpreter due to her fluency in English. When instructed to complete chores, Amelia had begun talking back to her parents, rolling her eyes, and using profanity. In one of these instances, her mother used the back of her hand to slap Amelia's mouth (i.e., *tapa boca*). At school later, Amelia's teacher made a report of potential physical abuse due to the state of Amelia's mouth after the *tapa boca*, as Amelia wore braces, and her lip caught on them and bled. Amelia's teacher may have been concerned about her well-being and wanted to ensure her safety. Teachers are also mandated to report suspected harm to children, so she may also have had concerns about legal ramifications if she didn't report the behavior. While we would not want to dissuade professionals from honoring their mandated reporting duties, we would encourage them to review any notable reporting trends. Given the overrepresentation of communities of color in the child protective system, examining any biases that may lead to reporting some families over others is critical to our feminist- and multicultural-centered efforts.

Additionally, after reporting, it would be useful for the teacher to refer Amelia to the school guidance counselor, who could speak with Amelia about the *tapa boca* and determine her level of fear and distress, which should inform the treatment process. If the guidance counselor also considered the value of *respeto*, they could develop a more nuanced understanding of the role of obedience and respect children are expected to show adults in Latinx families. As a result, the guidance counselor might have come away with a different view of the mother's interaction with Amelia that led to the *tapa boca*, and might be in a better position to help the family manage their acculturative and familial stressors as well as their communication patterns.

Additionally, Amelia's guidance counselor could also consult with her family and discuss their views as well as their potential needs. Making a report to child welfare services may have undermined the mother's power within the family as the matriarch, who has a responsibility to instill and uphold the family's cultural values. Making an abuse report may also result in an imbalance of power for the family and create a feeling that their cultural beliefs regarding appropriate child discipline have been labeled as "wrong." If Amelia's guidance counselor and teacher do not have a thorough understanding of Latinx values regarding child rearing, we recommend that they seek consultation on this topic to help them provide more culturally competent care for the students. In this case, it is more important to help the family develop disciplinary strategies that obey the law, preserve relationships, and honor cultural values. These three efforts are not mutually exclusive.

Amelia's role as the family's interpreter may create tension within the family, particularly if Amelia has adopted and exhibits values consistent with the dominant teenage culture in the United States. She may feel embarrassed at having to help her parents and may have been the subject of racial microaggressions by people who do not value or respect her family's status as first-generation immigrants. We recommend that those involved with Amelia's case inquire about the family's interest in accessing consistent and adequate interpretation services outside of the family. This may serve to reduce tension between Amelia and her parents and promote more harmonious interactions.

Alternatively, from a feminist perspective, it is important to pause and reflect on the forces that make striking a child acceptable, regardless of race, ethnicity, or class. Through this book's lens, the *tapa boca* is indicative of a greater issue. In the United States, the physical discipline of children is condoned. All other classes of people in the nation are protected from physical discipline by laws except children. And this practice is not just limited to families. In over nineteen states, school corporal punishment is still permitted with over 160 thousand children a year experiencing corporal punishment (Gershoff & Font, 2016).

Moreover, in Latin America, physical discipline is a common household practice, with two out of three children under the age of five being subjected to harsh and violent discipline (UNICEF, 2018). In order to eradicate this practice, UNICEF advises "the total prohibition of corporal punishment in all areas; [we] support the implementation of multi-sectoral programs and policies to promote positive parenting; promote norms, values and community mechanisms that support parenting without violence; and generate data and evidence to inform policy and measure progress towards the elimination of 'violent discipline.'" Again, a multi-pronged approach is necessary to prevent or reduce child maltreatment, involving not only relational efforts, but community and societal interventions as well.

The Case of Marco

We introduced Marco as an Afro-Caribbean, Cuban male who practiced a religion called Palo and whose teacher called child protective services after observing scarring on his shoulders. These scars were created as part of a rite of passage initiating Marco as a man. When asked about the scars, Marco indicated that he was not permitted to share their origin. In Marco's case, we see an ethical dilemma, as there is a conflict between the legal requirements teachers face to report abuse, and Marco's family's religious beliefs and practices. The American Academy of Pediatrics has called for the repeal of religious exemptions among all states to ensure that every child is protected under the law (American Academy of Pediatrics, 2013), so the legal obligation for Marco's teacher is to ensure that he is safe. However, if the teacher or a guidance counselor had talked to Marco's family, they would have had the opportunity to learn more about his religious beliefs and the context under which the scarring occurred.

In this case, as in the case of Amelia, we recommend that the teacher indicate to Marco that she is concerned for his well-being and make a referral to the guidance counselor or a community therapist. This clinician could then speak with his family regarding the scarring. Marco may have been able to adhere to the sacredness of his religion while still telling the teacher or a clinician that although he cannot share specifics, he engaged in the practice willingly and does not fear for his safety. Even then, depending on the state in which Marco and his family live, the teacher or the clinician might still be obligated to contact child protective services to report physical abuse. As it happened, Marco, his family, and his community experienced notable distress as a result of the report being made. In line with the recommendation to engage in a dialogue with Marco's family, we further recommend that the teacher and counselor acknowledge the differences between their own and Marco's family's cultural backgrounds and worldviews. Practicing cultural humility may not result in a different outcome in terms of someone having to make the report, but it would provide respect to the family by acknowledging the ethical dilemma, which could contribute to a different emotional experience for the family.

Viewing Marco's scarring as abusive stems from a U.S.-based bias that devalues the profound importance of the scarification ritual to Marco and his family. Prevailing U.S.-based religious ideologies that promote condemnation, fear, and an eternal existence in "hell" might also be deemed by some as equally problematic. Therefore, we also recommend that Marco's teacher and counselor consider the family's level of acculturation and ethnic-racial socialization, as these variables may impact Marco's and his family's understanding of the potential ramifications of his scarring being observed at school. If the teacher and counselor take these factors into account, in combination with having a direct conversation with the family, Marco, his parents, and their community members may be able to identify ways that he can follow his religious beliefs and uphold the cultural significance of the ritual without experiencing legal consequences.

Utilizing feminist principles, practitioners can deconstruct the role of religion in the lives of individuals, families, and communities. While research suggests that religion or spirituality has a protective quality, promoting resilience and optimal functioning (Brewer-Smyth & Koenig, 2014; Brooks et al., 2018), Karl Marx argued that religion was often used to promote inequality or maintain the status quo (Wolff & Leopold, 2021). In this particular case, it is important to discuss the role of religion in their lives with Marco and his family in ways that build consciousness, minimize oppression, and promote liberation, allowing for the construction of a narrative that is developed and embraced by the family.

The Case of Jaquann

We met Jaquann as a fifteen-year-old Black male who developed symptoms of posttraumatic stress after being robbed at gunpoint, and subsequently missed a substantial amount of school. When he contacted his school about making up his work to ensure his continued education, his guidance counselor expressed that she thought he had dropped out of school. His teacher committed a racial microaggression against Jaquann by presuming that his absences from school indicated that he was disinterested at best or engaged in delinquent behavior at worst. The counselor may have made further assumptions that his mother was uninvolved or was aware but unconcerned about Jaquann's absences, rather than recognizing that she was working to provide for the family's basic needs. We recommend that the guidance counselor contact Jaquann and his mother regarding the absences rather than waiting for him to follow up with them. This simple act might have garnered insight into the context involved in his situation. It is also possible that Jaquann, his mother, or both would not have felt comfortable disclosing the real reason for his absences to the guidance counselor; however, the assumption that he had withdrawn from school prevented the counselor from trying to learn more.

Furthermore, we recommend that Jaquann's guidance counselor and other school staff engage in self-examination and review the school's policies to determine, on an individual level, what drove the counselor's assumptions about Jaquann, and on a broader, more systemic level, what their school (and perhaps the whole district) can do to better support students of color. Without doing this evaluation, the counselor and the school will continue to hold and promote negative stereotypes (Sue et al., 2007) of students who may need help. The guidance counselor and school administrators should pursue relationships with local officials (e.g., the Mayor's office, city council, and local police) to address the systemic factors that are associated with this case. Jaquann's neighborhood would benefit from financial stabilization, equitable access to employment and educational opportunities, and other supports for parents and families (Haas et al., 2018).

The Case of Miguelina

We introduced Miguelina as a fourteen-year-old Mexican American girl who experienced chronic sexual abuse from her older brother. When the parents learned of the abuse, they sent her brother to Mexico to live with family members. As treatment progressed, the psychologist working with Miguelina learned that intimate partner violence and emotional abuse were also occurring within the family. It would be important for a clinician working with Miguelina to take into consideration the potential impact of a variety of factors, including intersectionality of different aspects of Miguelina's individual identity, acculturation level, recency of the family's immigration to the United States, and experiences with racism on micro and macro levels. As an individual identifying as female, Miguelina has likely experienced prioritizing of male perspectives and experiences in society and in her family. In the context of cultural values, such as *respeto,* Miguelina may have learned to uphold her family's preferences for level of privacy and concern for potential implications of the sexual abuse becoming more publicly known. This may lead her to be less willing to speak about the sexual or emotional abuse in the context of treatment. Furthermore, her parents may be less likely to view her father's behavior towards her as abusive, if they hold more traditional values.

It is recommended that the mental health clinician working with Miguelina's family assess the individual and cultural factors noted above. Without having this contextualized understanding of Miguelina and her family, the clinician risks implementing treatment in more of a "one size fits all" approach, which could contribute to the family's early withdrawal from treatment. It is also recommended that the clinician learn about Miguelina's strengths and values, as well as those of her family, and incorporate them into treatment selection and planning. Family based treatments, such as Culturally Modified Trauma-Focused Cognitive Behavioral Therapy (CM-TF-CBT) and Functional Family Therapy (FFT) draw on these strengths and values to increase the family's investment in treatment and motivation to complete it. Drawing on not only individual and family strengths, but also those in the community, is important to provide a treatment approach that more fully integrates various aspects of Miguelina's lived experience. Considering these factors while developing the treatment plan allows the clinician to work with Miguelina towards a sense of "radical healing." This notion of radical healing centers the dialectic of resisting oppressive factors while also moving towards freedom from those forces (French et al., 2020). For Miguelina, she may find oppression and strength within her family and it is recommended that her clinician assess her perceptions of their sources and potential implications for her treatment.

Case Discussions

As we conclude our work with the cases, our ultimate aim is to leave these clients and families with useful tools that will facilitate their optimal functioning, as advised in chapter 4. If the feminist and multicultural principles discussed throughout this book are properly implemented, clients should leave treatment embracing new narratives that are more nuanced and strengths based.

In the cases of Amelia, Bashiir, Marco, Jaquann, and Miguelina, the families should leave treatment with a deeper understanding of and appreciation for their cultural backgrounds, recognizing the thin narratives imposed on them by oppressive forces, and being able to expand their own narratives based on their values and goals. If practitioners involved have truly shared power, all of the clients will know how to properly advocate for themselves should they desire to do so, having broadened their knowledge around their rights, expanded their consciousness, leveraged appropriate familial and community resources, and acquired skills for effective communication and problem solving.

Specifically, in the case of Jaquann, the client and family would have received culturally adapted treatment that assisted them with addressing their trauma and adopting skills they can utilize with current and future challenges. Moreover, the family should leave treatment with a deeper understanding of the community and societal factors that contribute toward their distress and with the suitable connections in the neighborhood for addressing these problematic forces. Self-advocacy skills may be particularly relevant and useful in instances where the clients in the cases mentioned in this book find that some necessary resources are not present or are not easily accessible due to systemic racism and oppressive forces. In all the cases, the African proverb, *it takes a village*, is clearly germane. In short, leaving clients with tools that promote self-determination and engage natural supports is key.

A Practitioner's Perspective

During graduate school, I remember learning about the importance of highlighting ethnic, cultural, and identity related differences between myself and the client, as we examined ways that these differences may impact how we view a situation. I recall a clinical supervisor providing feedback to the group of supervisees that we should ask questions such as, "What is it like to share that with me as a White woman?" Although I knew he was right and intellectually—I understood the rationale—I felt uncomfortable doing this. Maybe I thought that highlighting our differences would create a gap and make the client feel that I did not understand or could not help. As I've grown as a clinician and worked with many families who may look, value, or love differently than I do, I recognize now the utmost importance of doing what my supervisor had suggested. I can think of times that highlighting, valuing, and inquiring about our differences has made a significant impact on treatment with individuals or families with whom I have worked. Instead of creating the gap I feared, it created a more authentic environment where (it seemed) the client felt better able to express their genuine concerns. I have seen a Black male patient exhale with apparent relief when I said "As a White woman, I have never had to fear for my life when interacting with a police officer." And when I worried that the client would think I could not understand a particular experience, I should not have worried—that was correct. Acknowledging that and inviting the client to share their reactions has made for what seems to be a better therapeutic relationship and outcome. Although I feel that I have grown in multicultural competence as a clinician, I understand that this is a lifelong journey that I am committed to traveling with an open heart and mind. — Renee L. DeBoard-Lucas

Closing Summary

This book utilizes concepts of feminism and multiculturalism to explore factors that contribute to and protect children from experiencing child maltreatment. By doing so, the authors have sought to identify strengths, examine variables that are associated with power differences between families and clinicians, and incorporate tools for social justice that can serve to prevent and respond to child maltreatment. Multicultural factors are crucial when considering whether a child has experienced abuse or neglect or if instead, their family has beliefs or practices that are just unfamiliar to their clinician. In a time when a global pandemic is disproportionately impacting families of color and police brutality continues to claim the lives of Black men, women, and children, it is paramount that clinicians and other service providers continue to do their part in showing that we can do better. Assessing and respecting diversity in values, experiences, and behaviors are steps on that path. Treating the child, family, and community are all important in preventing and responding to child maltreatment. What follows are resources and readings intended to provide additional tools to clinicians as they strive to support their clients as whole people, within their cultural contexts and values.

Recommended Resources by Topic

Childhood Trauma
  Sue, D. W., C. Z. Calle, N. Mendez, S. Alsaidi, & E. Glaeser. 2021. *Microintervention Strategies: What You Can Do to Disarm and Dismantle Individual and Systemic Racism and Bias.* Hoboken, NJ: Wiley.
  Van der Kolk, B. A. 2014. *The Body Keeps the Score: Brain, Mind, and Body in the Healing of Trauma.* New York, NY: Viking.
Child Maltreatment
  Bar-Lev, A., dir. (2014) 2015. *Happy Valley.* eVideo. New York: A&E IndieFilms.
  Child Welfare Information Gateway. 2016–present. Child Welfare Information Gateway Podcast Series. https://www.childwelfare.gov /more-tools-resources/podcast/.
  Fontes, L. A. 2008. *Child Abuse and Culture: Working with Diverse Families.* New York: Guilford Press.
  Goldthwait, B., dir. 2015. *Call Me Lucky.* eVideo. San Francisco: MPI Media Group.
  Harris, N. B. 2014. "How Childhood Trauma Affects Health Across a Lifetime." Video. TEDMED 2014. https://www.ted.com/talks /nadine_burke_harris_how_childhood_trauma_affects_health _across_a_lifetime.
  Kendall-Tackett, K. A. 2004. *Health Consequences of Abuse in the Family: A Clinical Guide for Evidence-Based Practice.* American

Psychological Association (APA) PsychNet. https://doi.org/10.1037 /10674-000. (Application and practice in health psychology.)

Knappenberger, B. & Marson, E., prod. 2020. *The Trials of Gabriel Fernandez*. Netflix series. Los Angeles: Luminant Media; San Francisco: Common Sense Media.

Koenig, L. J., L.S. Doll, A. E. O'Leary, & W. E. Pequegnat. 2004. *From Child Sexual Abuse to Adult Sexual Risk: Trauma, Revictimization, and Intervention*. APA PsychNet. https://doi.org/10.1037/10785-000.

Korbin, J., & R. Krugman, eds. 2014. *Handbook of Child Maltreatment*. Child Maltreatment Series. Dordrecht: Springer.

Myers, J.E.B. 2011. *The APSAC Handbook on Child Maltreatment*. Los Angeles: SAGE.

Miller-Perrin, C. L., & R. D. Perrin. 2013. *Child Maltreatment: An Introduction*. 3rd Edition. Thousand Oaks, CA: Sage Publications.

Noonan, K., dir. 2017. *Heal*. DVD. Beverly Hills, CA: Elevative Entertainment; Hillsboro, OR: Beyond Words Publishing.

Redford, J., dir. 2015. *Paper Tigers*. Film. Branford, CT: KPJR Films; Sausalito, CA: Ro*Co Films.

Warner, S. 2009. *Understanding the Effects of Child Sexual Abuse: Feminist Revolutions in Theory, Research and Practice*. New York: Routledge.

Child Wellness

American Academy of Pediatrics. 2006. *Connected Kids: Safe, Strong, Secure Clinical Guide*. Elk Grove Village, IL: American Academy of Pediatrics. https://depts.washington.edu/dbpeds/Screening%20Tools /ConnectedKids(AAP).pdf.

Hagan, J. F., J. S. Shaw, & P. M. Duncan. 2017. *Bright Futures: Guidelines for Health Supervision of Infants, Children, and Adolescents*. 4th edition. Elk Grove Village, IL: Bright Futures and the American Academy of Pediatrics.

Musalo, K., L. Frydman, & P. C. Cernadas. 2015. *Childhood and Migration in Central and North America: Causes, Policies, Practices and Challenges*. San Francisco: Center for Gender & Refugee Studies (CGRS); Buenos Aires: Migration and Asylum Program, Justice and Human Rights Center. https://cgrs.uchastings.edu/sites /default/files/Childhood_Migration_HumanRights_FullBook _English.pdf.

Cognitive Behavioral Therapy (CBT)

Cohen, J. A., A. P. Mannarino, & E. Deblinger. 2006. *Treating Trauma and Traumatic Grief in Children and Adolescents*. New York: Guilford Press. (A general treatment manual.)

Cohen, J. A., A. P. Mannarino, & E. Deblinger, E. 2012. *Treating Trauma and Traumatic Grief in Children and Adolescents*. New York: Guilford Press. (Describes treatment applications with culturally diverse populations.)

Cultural Competence

American Medical Association (AMA). N.d. Health Equity. https://www.ama-assn.org/delivering-care/health-equity. (Medical approach.)

APA. 2017. *Multicultural Guidelines: An Ecological Approach to Context, Identity, and Intersectionality*. Washington, DC: American Psychological Association. https://www.apa.org/about/policy/multicultural-guidelines.pdf. (Psychological approach.)

Clauss-Ehlers, C. S., S. J. Hunter, G. A. Morse, & P. Tummala-Narra. 2021. *Applying Multiculturalism: An Approach to the APA Guidelines*. Washington, DC: American Psychological Association. (An overview.)

National Association of Social Workers (NASW). 2015. *Standards and Indicators for Cultural Competence in Social Work Practice*. Washington, DC: National Association of Social Workers. https://www.socialworkers.org/LinkClick.aspx?fileticket=7dVckZAYUmk%3D&portalid=0. (Social Work approach.)

Racism and Anti-Racism

American Council on Education (ACE). 2019. "A Discussion About Race at ACE2019 with Beverly Daniel Tatum and Robin DiAngelo." YouTube video. https://www.youtube.com/watch?v=Zsxy_ah6g2A. (On equity in higher education.)

Banaji, M. R. & A. G. Greenwald. 2013. *Blindspot: Hidden Biases of Good People*. New York: Delacorte Press.

"Facing the Divide: Psychology's Conversation on Race and Health." https://www.apa.org/education-career/undergrad/diversity.

Helms, J. E. 2019. *A Race Is a Nice Thing to Have: A Guide to Being a White Person or Understanding the White Persons in Your Life*. 3rd edition. San Diego, CA: Cognella.

Henny, A. 2019–present. *Combing the Roots with Ally Henny*. Podcast series. https://combingtheroots.fireside.fm/.

Kendi, I. X. 2021. *Be Antiracist with Ibram X. Kendi*. Podcast series. New York: iHeartRadio; n.p.: Pushkin Industries. https://www.ibramxkendi.com/be-antiracist-podcast.

———. 2019. *How to Be an Anti-Racist*. New York: One World.

New York Times. 2019. *1619*. Podcast hosted by Nikole Hannah-Jones. https://www.nytimes.com/2020/01/23/podcasts/1619-podcast.html.

MSNBC. 2020. Chris Hayes Podcast with Nikole Hannah-Jones & Ibram X. Kendi. *Why Is This Happening?* Episode 84. YouTube audio. https://www.youtube.com/watch?v=_9h9WuSCdRs.

Perry, B. D., & M. Szalavitz. 2006. *The Boy Who Was Raised as a Dog and Other Stories from a Child Psychiatrist's Notebook: What Traumatized Children Can Teach Us about Loss, Love, And Healing*. New York: Basic Books.

Seattle Channel. 2018. "Dr. Robin DiAngelo discusses 'White Fragility'."
    YouTube audio. https://www.youtube.com/watch?v=45ey4jgoxeU.
Steele, C. M. 2011. *Whistling Vivaldi: How Stereotypes Affect Us and
    What We Can Do*. New York: W. W. Norton & Company, Inc.
We recommend the following frameworks, projects, and associations that
    provide a basic understanding of some issues around child
    maltreatment.
APA Division 44: Society for the Psychology of Sexual Orientation and
    Gender Diversity. N.d. https://www.apadivisions.org/division-44.
———. N.d. LGBTQ Psychology Resources. https://www.apadivisions
    .org/division-44/resources.
———. 2021. *APA Resolution on Gender Identity Change Efforts*.
    https://www.apa.org/about/policy/resolution-gender-identity-change
    -efforts.pdf.
APA Division 45: Society for the Psychological Study of Culture,
    Ethnicity, and Race. N.d. http://division45.org/.
APA Division 53: Society of Clinical Child and Adolescent Psychology.
    N.d. https://sccap53.org/.
APA Division 56: Trauma Psychology. N.d. https://www
    .apatraumadivision.org/.
Falicov, C. J. 2014. "Multidimensional Ecosystemic Comparative
    Approach (MECA)." In *Encyclopedia of Couple and Family Therapy*,
    edited by J. Lebow, A. Chambers, & D. Breunlin. Springer, Cham.
    https://doi.org/10.1007/978-3-319-15877-8_848-1. (MECA can be a
    resource for learning ways to identify, challenge, and dismantle
    systems of oppression. This approach includes a focus on social justice
    and cultural diversity and incorporates factors such as migration,
    acculturation, ecological contexts, family organization, and family
    life cycle.)
French, H., et al. 2020. "Toward a Psychological Framework of Radical
    Healing in Communities of Color." *The Counseling Psychiatrist* 48,
    no. 1: 14–46. (This framework draws on multiple approaches to
    inform clinical work, research, training programs, and advocacy for
    social justice. The approaches included are liberation psychology,
    Black psychology, ethnopolitical psychology, and intersectionality
    theory.)
National Child Traumatic Stress Network (NCTSN). N.d. https://www
    .nctsn.org/. (This network of agencies was designed to raise the
    quality of trauma-informed services and to increase individuals' and
    families' access to that care. Some of the services offered by NCTSN
    include providing evidenced-based trauma interventions, developing
    and disseminating treatments and resources for clinicians and the
    public, providing education on trauma-related topics, collaborating
    with other trauma-informed agencies, informing public policy, and
    raising awareness of trauma and its effects, among others.)

University of Pittsburgh. N.d. Open Door Project. http://opendoor.pitt
.edu. (Developed at the University of Pittsburgh, the Open Door
Project offers trainings and discusses on topics such as cultural
humility, multiculturalism, and social justice.)

We recommend the Violence Against Women and Children series by
Rutgers University Press, in which this book appears. The current
book focuses on broader concepts related to feminism and multiculturalism in the context of child maltreatment. Other books in the
series explore interventions suited for specific populations. Implementing treatments designed or adapted for a particular culture
provides the most effective, efficient, and ethical care. https://www
.rutgersuniversitypress.org/search-list?series=violence-against-women
-and-children.

Calzada, E., Faulkner, M., LaBrenz, C., & Fuentes, M. A. (2022).
*Preventing Child Maltreatment in the US: The Latinx Community
Perspective.* New Brunswick, NJ: Rutgers University Press.

Phillips, M., Moore, S, & Fuentes, M. A. (2022). *Preventing Child
Maltreatment in the US: The Black Community Perspective.* New
Brunswick, NJ: Rutgers University Press.

Ross, R., Greene, J., & Fuentes, M. A. (2022). *Preventing Child Maltreatment in the US: The American Indian and Alaska Native Perspectives.*
New Brunswick, NJ: Rutgers University Press.

References

Alexander, A. 2017. "Social Justice, Advocacy, and Early Career Practice." *Psychotherapy Bulletin* 52, no. 4. https://societyforpsychotherapy.org /social-justice-advocacy-and-early-career-practice/.

Alexander, J., and B. Parsons. 1982. "Understanding the Principles of Family Functioning." In *Functional Family Therapy: Principles and Procedures*, 9–33. N.p.: Brooks/Cole Publishing Company.

Alexander, J. F., H. B. Waldron, M. S. Robbins, and A. A. Neeb. 2013. *Functional Family Therapy for Adolescent Behavior Problems*. Washington, DC: American Psychological Association.

Altafim, E.R.P., and M.B.M. Linhares. 2016. "Universal Violence and Child Maltreatment Prevention Programs for Parents: A Systemic Review." *Psychosocial Intervention* 25, no. 1: 27–38.

American Academy of Pediatrics, Committee on Bioethics. 2013. "Conflicts between Religious and Spiritual Beliefs and Pediatric Care: Informed Refusal, Exemptions, and Public Funding." *Pediatrics* 132, no. 5: 962–965.

American Association for Marriage and Family Therapy. 2015. Code of Ethics. https://www.aamft.org/Legal_Ethics/Code_of_Ethics.aspx.

American Counseling Association (ACA). 2014. *The ACA 2014 Code of Ethics*. https://www.counseling.org/resources/aca-code-of-ethics.pdf. Alexandra, VA: American Counseling Association.

American Psychological Association, Presidential Task Force on Evidence-Based Practice. 2006. Evidence-Based Practice in Psychology. *American Psychologist* 61, no. 4: 271–285.

American Psychological Association (APA). 2008. Children and Trauma: Update for Mental Health Professionals. Produced by the 2008 Presidential Task Force on Posttraumatic Stress Disorder and Trauma in Children and Adolescents. https://www.apa.org/pi/families/resources/children -trauma-update.

———. 2009. *Effective Strategies to Support Positive Parenting in Community Health Centers: Report of the Working Group on Child Maltreatment*

Prevention in Community Health Centers. https://www.apa.org/pi /prevent-violence/resources/positive-parenting-summary.pdf. Washington, DC: American Psychological Association.

———. 2013. "Crossroads: The Psychology of Immigration in the New Century." *Journal of Latina/o Psychology* 1, no. 3:133–148.

———. 2017a. Ethical Principles of Psychologists and Code of Conduct. https://www.apa.org/ethics/code/.

———. 2017b. *Multicultural Guidelines: An Ecological Approach to Context, Identity, and Intersectionality.* http://www.apa.org/about/policy /multicultural-guidelines.pdf.

———. 2018. Statement of APA President Regarding the Traumatic Effects of Separating Immigrant Families. Press release. https://www.apa.org /news/press/releases/2018/05/separating-immigrant-families.

———. 2019. Resolution on Physical Discipline of Children by Parents. https://www.apa.org/about/policy/physical-discipline.pdf.

———. 2020. *Advocacy Impact: 2020 American Psychological Association Advocacy Priorities.* https://www.apaservices.org/advocacy/2020 -advocacy-priorities.pdf.

———. 2021a. *Corporal Punishment Does Not Belong in Public Schools.* https://votervoice.s3.amazonaws.com/groups/apaadvocacy/attachments /APA_Corporal_Punishment_Fact-Sheet.pdf.

———. 2021b. *APA Resolution on Gender Identity Change Efforts.* https:// www.apa.org/about/policy/resolution-gender-identity-change-efforts .pdf.

Anderson, V., S. Boddapati, and S. Pate. 2019. "Prevention and Promotion." In *Introduction to Community Psychology: Becoming an Agent of Change,* edited by Leonard A. Jason, Olya Glantsman, Jack F. O'Brien, and Kaitlyn N. Ramian, 221–242. Chicago: DePaul University College of Science and Health Full Text Publications. https://via.library.depaul.edu /cshtextbooks/1.

Anzaldúa, G. E. 2012. *Borderlands/La Frontera: The New Mestiza.* 4th ed. San Francisco: Aunt Lute Books.

Arruabarrena, I., and J. De Paúl. 2012. "Early Intervention Programs for Children and Families: Theoretical and Empirical Bases Supporting Their Social and Economic Efficiency." *Psychosocial Intervention* 21, no. 2: 117–127.

Atkinson, D. R., C. E. Thompson, and S. K. Grant. 1993. "A Three-Dimensional Model for Counseling Ethnic Minorities." In *Counseling American Minorities: A Cross-Cultural Perspective,* edited by D. Atkinson, G. Morten, and D. Sue. Madison. WI: Brown & Benchmark.

Bailey, A. M., A. M. Brazil, A. Conrad-Hiebner, and J. Counts. 2015. "Protective Factors among Latino Families Involved with Child Welfare: A Review of Spanish Protective Factors on Child Maltreatment in Seven Countries." *Children and Youth Services Review* 55: 93–102.

Banaji, M. R., and A. G. Greenwald. 2016. *Blind Spot: Hidden Biases of Good People.* New York: Bantam Books.

Bandini, E., A. D. Fisher, V. Ricca, J. Ristori, M. C. Meriggiola, E. A. Jannini, et al. 2011. "Childhood Maltreatment in Subjects with Male-To-Female Gender Identity Disorder." *International Journal of Impotence Research* 23, no. 6: 276–285.

Belsky, J. 1980. "Child Maltreatment: An Ecological Integration." *American Psychologist* 35, no. 4: 320–335.

Bernard, K., T. Lind, and M. Dozier. 2014. "Neurobiological Consequences of Neglect and Abuse." In *Handbook of Child Maltreatment*, edited by Richard D. Krugman and Jill E. Korbin, 205–223. New York: Springer Nature.

Bernstein, K.M., C. J. Najdowski, and K. S. Wahrer. 2020. "Racial Stereo-typing and Misdiagnosis of Child Abuse." *Monitor on Psychology* 51, no. 5 (July): 35.

Berry, J.W. 2005. "Acculturation: Living Successfully in Two Cultures." *International Journal of Intercultural Relations* 29, no. 6: 697–712.

BigFoot, D. S., and B. W. Funderburk. 2011. "Honoring Children, Making Relatives: The Cultural Translation of Parent-Child Interaction Therapy for American Indian and Alaskan Native Families." *Journal of Psychoactive Drugs* 43, no. 4: 309–318.

BigFoot, D. S., and S. R. Schmidt. 2013. "American Indian and Alaskan Native Children: Honoring Children—Mending the Circle." In *Trauma-Focused CBT for Children and Adolescents*, edited by J. A. Cohen, A. P. Mannarino., and E. Deblinger, 280–300. New York: Guilford Press.

Bjørseth, Å., and L. Wichstrøm. 2016. "Effectiveness of Parent-Child Interaction Therapy (PCIT) in the Treatment of Young Children's Behavior Problems. A Randomized Controlled Study." *PLoS One* 11, no. 9: 1–19.

Bochenek, M. G. (2019). "US: Family separation harming children, families." *Human Rights Watch*, July 11. https://www.hrw.org/news/2019/07/11/us-family-separation-harming-children-families.

Boyd-Franklin, N. 2013. *Black Families in Therapy: Understanding the African-American Experience*. 2nd ed. New York: Guilford Press.

Brewer-Smyth, K., and H. G. Koenig. 2014. "Could Spirituality and Religion Promote Stress Resilience in Survivors of Childhood Trauma?" *Issues in Mental Health Nursing* 35, no. 4: 251–256.

Bronfenbrenner, U. 1977. "Toward an Experimental Ecology of Human Development." *American Psychologist* 32: 513–531.

Brooks, F., V. Michaelson, N. King, J. Inchley, and W. Pickett. 2018. "Spirituality as a Protective Health Asset for Young People: An International Comparative Analysis from Three Countries." *International Journal of Public Health* 63, no. 3: 387–395.

Brown, L. S. 1994. *Subversive Dialogues: Theory in Feminist Therapy*. New York: Basic Books.

———. 2010. *Feminist Therapy*. Theories of Psychotherapy Series. Washington, DC: American Psychological Association.

———. 2018. "Introduction: Feminist Therapy—Not for Cisgender Women Only." *Feminist Therapy*, 2nd ed., 3–10. Theories of Psychotherapy Series. Washington, DC: American Psychological Association. The APA has made this text available online: https://www.apa.org/pubs/books/Feminist-Therapy-Chapter-1-Sample.pdf.

Bryant-Davis, T., and L. Comas-Díaz. 2016. "Introduction: Womanist and Mujerista Psychologies." In *Womanist and Mujerista Psychologies: Voices of Fire, Acts of Courage*, edited by T. Bryant-Davis and L. Comas-Díaz, 3–25. Washington, DC: American Psychological Association.

Brydon-Miller, M. D. Greenwood, and P. Maguire. 2003. "Why Action Research?" *Action Research* 1, no. 1: 9–28.

Calzada, E.J., Y. Fernandez, and D. E. Cortes. 2010. "Incorporating the Cultural Value of *Respeto* into a Framework of Latino Parenting." *Cultural Diversity and Ethnic Minority Psychology* 16, no. 1: 77–86.

Caughy M, O'Campo P, Randolph S, Nickerson K. (2002). The influence of racial socialization practices on the cognitive and behavioral competence of African-American preschoolers. *Child Development, 73*, 1611–1625.

Caughy M., S. Nettles, P. O'Campo, and K. Lohrfink. 2006. "Neighborhood Matters: Racial Socialization of African-American Children." *Child Development* 77: 1220–1236.

CBS News. 2021. "Biden Orders Department of Justice to Phase Out Contracts with Private Prisons." January 27. https://www.cbsnews.com/news/private-prisons-justice-department-biden-executive-order/.

Centers for Disease Control and Prevention (CDC). N.d.-a. Child Abuse and Neglect: Risk and Protective Factors. Accessed January 5, 2022. https://www.cdc.gov/violenceprevention/childabuseandneglect/riskprotectivefactors.html.

———. N.d.-b. Child Abuse and Neglect: Preventing Child Abuse and Neglect. Accessed January 6, 2022. https://www.cdc.gov/violenceprevention/childabuseandneglect/definitions.html.

———. N.d.-c. Childhood Obesity Facts. Accessed January 6, 2022. https://www.cdc.gov/obesity/data/childhood.html.

———. N.d.-d Demographic Trends of COVID-19 Cases and Deaths in the US Reported to CDC. Accessed January 6, 2022. https://www.cdc.gov/covid-data-tracker/index.html#demographics.

———. N.d.-e. Health Equity Considerations and Racial and Ethnic Minority Groups. Accessed January 6, 2022. https://www.cdc.gov/coronavirus/2019-ncov/community/health-equity/race-ethnicity.html.

———. N.d.-f. Adult Obesity Causes & Consequences. Accessed January 6, 2022. https://www.cdc.gov/obesity/adult/causes.html

———. N.d.-g. *Prevention*. Accessed January 6, 2022. https://www.cdc.gov/pictureofamerica/pdfs/Picture_of_America_Prevention.pdf.

Chaffin, M., J. F. Silovsky, B. Funderburk, L. A. Valle, E. V. Brestan, T. Balachova, et al. 2004. "Parent-Child Interaction Therapy with

Physically Abusive Parents: Efficacy for Reducing Future Abuse Reports." *Journal of Consulting and Clinical Psychology* 72, no. 3: 500–510.

Chavez, V. 2012. "Cultural Humility." YouTube video, 29:28. https://www .youtube.com/watch?v=SaSHLbS1V4w.

Chavez-Dueñas, N. Y., H. Y. Adames, J. G. Perez-Chavez, and S. P. Salas. 2019. "Healing Ethno-Racial Trauma in Latinx Immigrant Communities: Cultivating Hope, Resistance, and Action." *American Psychologist* 74, no. 1: 49–62.

Chen, M., and K. L. Chan. 2015. "Effects of Parenting Programs on Child Maltreatment Prevention: A Meta-analysis." *Trauma, Violence, & Abuse* 17, no. 1: 88–104.

Cheng, T. L., M. A. Emmanuel, D. J. Levy, and R. R. Jenkins. 2015. "Child Health Disparities: What Can a Clinician Do?" *Pediatrics* 136, no. 5: 961–968.

Child Welfare Information Gateway. 2016. *Racial Disproportionality and Disparity in Child Welfare.* U.S. Department of Health and Human Services, Children's Bureau.

———. 2018. *Acts of omission: An overview of child neglect.* U.S. Department of Health and Human Services, Children's Bureau. https://www.childwelfare .gov/pubs/focus/acts/

———. N.d. *About Child Welfare Information Gateway.* https://www.child welfare.gov/aboutus/

Child Trends. 2013. *Attitudes toward Spanking.* https://www.childtrends.org /wp-content/uploads/2015/01/indicator_1420212520.5577.html.

Cohen, J. A., and S. J. Cozza. 2013. "Children in Military Families." *Trauma-Focused CBT for Children and Adolescents*, 199–224. New York: Guilford Press.

Cohen, J. A., A. P. Mannarino, and E. Deblinger. 2006. *Treating Trauma and Traumatic Grief in Children and Adolescents.* New York: Guilford Press.

Comas-Díaz, L., G. N. Hall, and H. A. Neville. 2019. "Racial Trauma: Theory, Research, and Healing: Introduction to the Special Issue." *American Psychologist* 74, no. 1: 1–5.

Comas-Diaz, L., M. B. Lykes, and R. D. Alcaron. 1998. "Ethnic Conflict and the Psychology of Liberation in Guatemala, Peru, and Puerto Rico." *American Psychologist* 53, no. 7: 778–791.

Community Healing Network, Emotional Emancipation Circles, and the Association of Black Psychologists, Inc. 2016. *Family Care, Community Care and Self-Care Tool Kit: Healing in the Face of Cultural Trauma.* http://www.abpsi.org/pdf/FamilyCommunitySelfCareToolKit.pdf.

Corona, G., M. Monami, E. Fanni, A. Galleni, G. Forti, E. Mannucci, and M. Maggi. 2011. "Childhood Maltreatment in Subjects with Male-to-Female Gender Identity Disorder." *International Journal of Impotence Research* 23, no. 6: 276–285.

Crenshaw, K. 1989. "Demarginalizing the Intersection of Race and Sex: A Black Feminist Critique of Antidiscrimination Doctrine, Feminist Theory and Antiracist Politics." *University of Chicago Legal Forum*1989, Article 8.

Cross, W. E., Jr., T. A. Parham, and J. E. Helms. 1991. "The Stages of Black Identity Development: Nigrescence Models." In *Black Psychology*, edited by R. L. Jones, 319–338. N. p.: Cobb & Henry Publishers.

Cumming-Potvin, W. 2013. "'New basics' and Literacies: Deepening Reflexivity in Qualitative Research." *Qualitative Research Journal* 13, no. 2: 214–230.

DeAngelis, T. 2009. "Unmasking 'Racial Microaggressions'." *Monitor on Psychology* 40, no. 2: 42. This article is also available online. https://www.apa.org/monitor/2009/02/microaggression.aspx.

De Arellano, M. A., C. K. Danielson, and J. W. Felton. 2012. "Children of Latino Descent: Culturally Modified TF-CBT." In *Trauma-Focused CBT for Children and Adolescents: Treatment Applications*, edited by J. A. Cohen, A. P. Mannarino, and E. Deblinger, 253–279. New York: Guilford Press.

Deer, S. 2019. "(En) Gendering Indian Law: Indigenous Feminist Legal Theory in the United States." *Yale Journal of Law and Feminism* 31: 1–34.

Del Campo, A., and M. Fávero. 2020. "Effectiveness of Programs for the Prevention of Child Sexual Abuse: A Comprehensive Review of Evaluation Studies." *European Psychologist* 25, no. 1: 1–15.

DeMause, Lloyd. 2002. *The Emotional Life of Nations*. London: Karnac.

DePanfilis, D. 2006. *Child Neglect: A Guide for Prevention, Assessment and Intervention*. Washington, DC: U.S. Department of Health and Human Services Administration for Children and Families. https://www.childwelfare.gov/pubPDFs/neglect.pdf.

Devine, P. G., P. S, Forscher, A. J. Austin, and W. L. Cox. 2012. "Long-Term Reduction in Implicit Race Bias: A Prejudice Habit-Breaking Intervention." *Journal of Experimental Social Psychology* 48, no. 6: 1267–1278.

Draganović, S. 2011. "Approaches to Feminist Therapy: A Case Study Illustration." *Journal of Transdisciplinary Studies* 4, no. 1: 110–127.

Eyberg, S. 1988. "Parent-Child Interaction Therapy: Integration of Traditional and Behavioral Concerns." *Child & Family Behavior Therapy* 10, no. 1: 33–46.

Falicov, C. J. 2012. "Immigrant Family Processes: A Multidimensional Framework (MECA)." In *Normal Family Processes: Growing Diversity and Complexity*, 4th edition, edited by F. Walsh, 297–323. New York: Guilford Press.

———. (2013) 2014. *Latino Families in Therapy*, 2nd edition. New York: Guilford Press.

Falicov, C. J., and L. Brudner-White. 1983. "The Shifting Family Triangle: The Issue of Cultural and Contextual Relativity." In *Cultural*

Perspectives in Family Therapy, edited by C. J. Falicov, 51–67. N.p.: Aspen Publishing.

Featherstone, B., and B. Fawcett. 1994. "Feminism and Child Abuse: Opening Up Some Possibilities?" *Critical Social Policy* 14, no. 42: 61–80.

Federal Bureau of Investigation (FBI). 2019. 2019 Hate Crime Statistics. https://ucr.fbi.gov/hate-crime/2019/topic-pages/victims.

Fedina, L., C. Williamson, and T. Perdue. 2016. "Risk Factors for Domestic Child Sex Trafficking in the United States." *Journal of Interpersonal Violence* 34: 2653–2673.

Felitti, V. J., R. F. Anda, D. Nordenberg, D. F. Williamson, A. M. Spitz, V. Edwards, M. P. Koss, and J. S. Marks. 1998. "Relationship of Childhood Abuse and Household Dysfunction to Many of the Leading Causes of Death in Adults: The Adverse Childhood Experiences (ACE) Study." *American Journal of Preventive Medicine* 14, no. 4: 245–258.

———. 2019. "Relationship of Childhood Abuse and Household Dysfunction to Many of the Leading Causes of Death in Adults: The Adverse Childhood Experiences (ACE) Study." *American Journal of Preventive Medicine* 56, no. 6: 774–786.

Fentiman, L. C. 2017. Blaming Mothers: American Law and the Risks to Children's Health. NYU Press.

Finkelhor, D., A. Shattuck, H. A. Turner, and S. L. Hamby. 2014. "The Lifetime Prevalence of Child Sexual Abuse and Sexual Assault Assessed in Late Adolescence." *Journal of Adolescent Health* 55, no. 3: 329–333.

Fontes, L. A. 2005. *Child Abuse and Culture: Working with Diverse Families.* New York: Guilford Press.

Forscher, P. S., C. Mitamura, E. L. Dix, W.T.L. Cox, and P. G. Devine. 2017. "Breaking the Prejudice Habit: Mechanisms, Timecourse, and Longevity." *Journal of Experimental Social Psychology* 72: 133–146.

Fortson, B. L., J. Klevens, M. T. Merrick, K. L. Gilbert, and S. P. Alexander. 2016. *Preventing Child Abuse and Neglect: A Technical Package for Policy, Norm, and Programmatic Activities.* Atlanta, GA: Division of Violence Prevention, National Center for Injury Prevention and Control, and the Centers for Disease Control and Prevention. https://www.cdc.gov/violenceprevention/pdf/CAN-Prevention-Technical-Package.pdf.

Freire, P. 1993. *Pedagogy of the Oppressed.* New York: Continuum.

French, B. H., J. A. Lewis, D. V. Moslye, H. Y. Adames, N. Y. Chaves-Dueñas, G. A. Chen, and H. A. Neville. 2020. "Toward a Psychological Framework of Radical Healing in Communities of Color." *The Counseling Psychologist* 48, no. 1: 14–46.

Fuentes, M. A., and Adamés, H. Y. 2011. "The Socio-Cultural Profile (SCP)." In *Experiential Activities for Teaching Multicultural Counseling Classes and Infusing Cultural Diversity into Core Classes*, edited by M. Pope, J. Pangelinan, and A. Coker, 153–155. Alexandria, VA: American Counseling Association Press.

Fuentes, M. A., D. G. Zelaya, and J. W. Madsen. 2020. "Rethinking the Course Syllabus: Considerations for Promoting Equity, Diversity and Inclusion." *Teaching of Psychology* 48, no. 1: 69–79.

Funderburk, B. W., and S. M. Eyberg. 2011. "Parent-Child Interaction Therapy." In *History of Psychotherapy: Continuity and Change*, 2nd edition, edited by J. C. Norcross, G. R. VandenBos, and D. K. Freedheim, 415–420. Washington, DC: American Psychological Association.

Gale, M. M., A. L. Pieterse, D. L. Lee, K. Huynh, S. Powell, and K. Kirkinis. 2020. "A Meta-Analysis of the Relationship between Internalized Racial Oppression and Health-Related Outcomes." *The Counseling Psychologist* 48, no. 4: 498–525.

Gallardo, M. E. 2014. *Developing Cultural Humility: Embracing Race, Privilege and Power*. Thousand Oaks, CA: Sage.

Gearon, J. 2021. "Indigenous Feminism Is Our Culture." *Stanford Social Innovation Review*. February 11. https://doi.org/10.48558/WBFS-NM87.

Gershoff, E. T. 2013. "Spanking and Child Development: We Know Enough Now to Stop Hitting Our Children." *Child Development Perspectives* 7, no. 3: 133–137.

———. 2021. "APA and Division 37 Sponsor Congressional Briefing to Support Protecting Our Students in Schools Act." *The Advocate*. July. https://www.apadivisions.org/division-37/publications/newsletters/advocate/2021/07/end-violence-against-children.

Gershoff, E. T., and S. H. Bitensky. 2007. "The Case against Corporal Punishment of Children: Converging Evidence from Social Science Research and International Human Rights Law and Implications for U.S. Public Policy." *Psychology, Public Policy, and Law* 13, no. 4: 231–272.

Gershoff, E. T., and S. A. Font. 2016. "Corporal Punishment in US Public Schools: Prevalence, Disparities in Use, and Status in State and Federal Policy." *Social Policy Report* 30, no. 1: 1–26.

Gershoff, E. T., and A. Grogan-Kaylor. 2016. "Spanking and Child Outcomes: Old Controversies and New Meta-Analyses." *Journal of Family Psychology* 30, no. 4: 453–469.

Gershoff, E. T., G. S. Goodman, C. L. Miller-Perrin, G. W. Holden, Y. Jackson, and A. E. Kazdin. 2018. "The Strength of the Causal Evidence against Physical Punishment of Children and Its Implications for Parents, Psychologists, and Policymakers." *American Psychologist* 73, no. 5: 626–638.

Gershoff, E. T., K. M. Purtell, and I. Holas. 2015. "Corporal Punishment in U.S. Public Schools: Legal Precedents, Current Practices, and Future Policy." *Advances in Child and Family Policy and Practice*, 1–105. N.p.: SpringerLink.

Gibbs, A., N. Duvvury, and S. Scriver. 2017. *What Works Evidence Review: The Relationship between Poverty and Intimate Partner Violence*. N. p., UK: What Works to Prevent Violence Against Women and Girls Programme. https://static1.squarespace.com/static/5656cae6e4b00f1

88f3228ee/t/59e44e2da8b2b0193318387b/1508134448965/Poverty+IPV
+Evidence+Brief_new+copy.pdf.

Global Initiative to End All Corporal Punibshment of Children. 2018.
https://endcorporalpunishment.org/countdown/.

Global Partnership to End Violence Against Children. 2022. Ending
Corporal Punishment: End Violence. https://www.end-violence.org
/ending-corporal-punishment.

Golden, S. 2020. "Coronavirus in African Americans and Other People of
Color." Johns Hopkins Medicine. https://www.hopkinsmedicine.org
/health/conditions-and-diseases/coronavirus/covid19-racial-disparities.

Goldenberg, H., and I. Goldenberg. 2013. *Family Therapy: An Overview.*
N.p., United States: Brooks/Cole, Cengage Learning.

Goodman, L. A., B. Liang, J. E. Helms, R. E. Latta, E. Sparks, and
S. R. Weintraub. 2004. "Training Counseling Psychologists as Social
Justice Agents: Feminist and Multicultural Principles in Action."
Counseling Psychologist 32, no. 6: 793–836.

Goodman, L. A., K. F. Smyth, A. M. Borges, and R. Singer. 2009. "When
Crises Collide: How Intimate Partner Violence and Poverty Intersect to
Shape Women's Mental Health and Coping." *Trauma, Violence and
Abuse: Special Issue on the Mental Health Implications of Violence Against
Women* 10, no. 4: 306–329.

Brown, and E. Patten. 2018. "The Narrowing, but Persistent, Gender Gap in
Pay." Pew Research Center. https://medium.com/@pewresearch/the
-narrowing-but-persistent-gender-gap-in-pay-30777d55876e.

Haas, B. M., K. A. Berg, M. M. Schmidt-Sane, J. E. Korbin, and J. C. Spilsbury.
2018. "How Might Neighborhood Built Environment Influence Child
Maltreatment? Caregiver Perceptions." *Science & Social Medicine* 214:
171–178.

Hamby, S., D. Finkelhor, H. Turner, and R. Ormrod. 2010. "The Overlap of
Witnessing Partner Violence with Child Maltreatment and Other
Victimizations in a Nationally Representative Survey of Youth." *Child
Abuse & Neglect* 34, no. 10: 734–741.

Harris, M. S., and W. Hackett. 2008. "Decision Points in Child Welfare: An
Action Research Model to Address Disproportionality." *Children and
Youth Services Review* 30, no. 2: 199–215.

Hays, P. A. (2001). *Addressing Cultural Complexities in Practice: A Framework for Clinicians and Counselors.* 1st edition. Washington, DC:
American Psychological Association.

———. (2016). *Addressing Cultural Complexities in Practice: Assessment,
Diagnosis and Therapy.* 3rd edition. Washington, DC: American
Psychological Association.

Heidari, Z., T. D. Gissandaner, and J. F. Silovsky. 2018. "Differences in
Recruiting and Engaging Rural and Urban Families in Home-Based
Parenting Programs." *Journal of Rural Mental Health* 42, no. 2:
133–144.

Helms, J. E. 2019. *A Race Is a Nice Thing to Have: A Guide to Being a White Person or Understanding the White Persons in Your Life*. San Diego, CA: Cognella Academic Publishing.

Helms, J. E. (Ed.). 1990. *Black and White Racial Identity: Theory, Research, and Practice*. New York: Greenwood Press.

Henriques, G. 2015. "The Biopsychosocial Model and Its Limitations." *Psychology Today*. October 30. https://www.psychologytoday.com/us /blog/theory-knowledge/201510/the-biopsychosocial-model-and-its -limitations.

Herrenkohl, Todd, D. Higgins, M. Merrick, and R. Leeb. 2015. "Positioning a Public Health Framework at the Intersection of Child Maltreatment and Intimate Partner Violence: Primary Prevention Requires Working Outside Existing Systems." *Child Abuse & Neglect* 48: 22–28.

Hook, J. N., D. E. Davis, J. Owen, E. L. Worthington, and S. O. Utsey. 2013. "Cultural Humility: Measuring Openness to Culturally Diverse Clients." *Journal of Counseling Psychology* 60, no. 3: 353–366.

hooks, b. 2015. *Feminist Theory: From Margin to Center*. New York: Routledge.

Howard, J. A., and D. G. Renfrow. 2014. "Intersectionality." In *Handbook of the Social Psychology of Inequality*, edited by J. D. McLeod, E. J. Lawler, and M. Schwalbe, 95–121. N.p.: SpringerLink.

Howes, R. 2008. "Terminating Therapy, Part IV: How to Terminate." *Psychology Today*. October 30. https://www.psychologytoday.com/us /blog/in-therapy/200810/terminating-therapy-part-iv-how-terminate.

Hughes, D., J. Rodriguez, E. P. Smith, D. J. Johnson, H. C. Stevenson, and P. Spicer. 2006. "Parents' Ethnic-Racial Socialization Practices: A Review of Research and Directions for Future Study." *Developmental Psychology* 42, no. 5: 747–770.

Hymel, K. P., M. S. Dias, E. S. Halstead, M. Wang, V. M. Chinchilli, B. Herman, et al. 2018. "Racial and Ethnic Disparities and Bias in the Evaluation and Reporting of Abusive Head Trauma." *The Journal of Pediatrics* 198: 137–143.

Jason, L. A., O. Glantsman, J. F. O'Brien, and K. N. Ramian (Eds.). 2019. "Introduction to the Field of Community Psychology." In *Introduction to Community Psychology*, edited by the authors. Montreal: The Rebus Press. https://press.rebus.community/introductiontocommunitypsychology/.

Jasko, K., J. Pyrkosz-Pacyna, G. Czarnek, K. Dukala, and M. Szastok. 2020. "The STEM Graduate: Immediately after Graduation, Men and Women Already Differ in Job Outcomes, Attributions for Success, and Desired Job Characteristics." *Global Perspectives on Women and Work* 76, no. 3: 512–542.

Jones, C. P. 2000. "Levels of Racism: A Theoretic Framework and a Gardener's Tale." *American Journal of Public Health* 90, no. 8: 1212–1215.

Katz, M. S. 1976. *A History of Compulsory Education Laws*. Fastback Series No. 75, the Bicentennial Series. Bloomington, IN: Phi Delta Kappa Educational Foundation. https://files.eric.ed.gov/fulltext/ED119389.pdf.

Kavi, A. 2021. "A Court Filing Says Parents of 445 Separated Migrant Children Still Have Not Been Found." *New York Times*. April 7, updated October 28. https://www.nytimes.com/2021/04/07/us/migrant-children-separated-border.html.

Kiser, L. J. 2008. Strengthening Family Coping Resources: Multifamily Group for Families Impacted by Trauma. Unpublished manuscript.

Kolko, D. J. 1996a. "Individual Cognitive-Behavioral Treatment and Family Therapy for Physically Abused Children and Their Offending Parents: A Comparison of Clinical Outcomes." *Child Maltreatment: Journal of the American Professional Society on the Abuse of Children* 1, no. 4: 322–342.

———. 1996b. "Clinical Monitoring of Treatment Course in Child Physical Abuse: Psychometric Characteristics and Treatment Comparisons." *Child Abuse & Neglect* 20, no. 1: 23–43.

Kolko, D. J., A. M. Iselin, and K. Gully. 2011. "Evaluation of the Sustainability and Clinical Outcome of Alternatives for Families: A Cognitive-Behavioral Therapy (AF-CBT) in a Child Protection Center." *Child Abuse & Neglect* 35, no. 2: 105–116.

Korbin, J. E., and R. D. Krugman (Eds.). 2014. *Handbook of Child Maltreatment*. New York: Springer.

Krugman, S. D., and W. G. Lane. 2014. "Fatal Child Abuse." In *Handbook of Child Maltreatment*, edited by J. E. Korbin and R. D. Krugman, 99–112. New York: Springer.

LaRoche, M. J., and A. Maxie. 2003. "Ten Considerations in Addressing Cultural Differences in Psychotherapy." *Professional Psychology: Research and Practice* 34, no. 2: 180–186.

Ladson-Billing, G., and W. F. Tate. 1995. "Toward Critical Race Theory in Education." *Teachers College Record* 97, no. 1: 47–68.

Lancaster, E., and J. Lumb. 1999. "Bridging the Gap: Feminist Theory and Practice Reality in Work with the Perpetrators of Child Sexual Abuse." *Child and Family Social Work* 4: 119–130.

Lane, W. G., D. M. Rubin, R. Monteith, and C. W. Christian. 2002. "Racial Differences in the Evaluation of Pediatric Fractures for Physical Abuse." *JAMA* 288, no. 13: 1603–1609.

Lanier, P., P. L. Kohl, J. Benz, D. Swinger, and B. Drake. 2014. "Preventing Maltreatment with a Community-Based Implementation of Parent-Child Interaction Therapy." *Journal of Child & Family Studies* 23, no. 2: 449–460.

Lansford, J. E., L. Chang, K. A. Dodge, P. S. Malone, P. Oburu, K. Palmérus, et al. 2005. "Physical Discipline and Children's Adjustment: Cultural Normativeness as a Moderator." *Child Development* 76, 1234–1246.

Lefebvre, R., B. Fallon, M. Van Wert, and J. Filippelli. 2017. "Examining the Relationship between Economic Hardship and Child Maltreatment Using Data from the Ontario Incidence Study of Reported Child Abuse and Neglect—2013." *Behavioral Science* 7, no. 1: 6.

Leineman, C. C., L. A. Brabson, A. Highlander, N. M. Wallace, and C. B. McNeil. 2017. "Parent–Child Interaction Therapy: Current Perspectives." *Psychology Research and Behavior Management* 10: 239–256.

Longley, R. 2020. "Womanist: Definition and Examples." ThoughtCo. https://www.thoughtco.com/womanist-feminism-definition-3528993.

Maguire-Jack, K., and T. Negash. 2016. "Parenting Stress and Child Maltreatment: The Buffering Effect of Neighborhood Social Service Availability and Accessibility." *Children & Youth Services Review* 60: 27–33.

Marans, S., H. Hahn, C. Epstein and N. Arnow. (2012). *The Safe Horizon-Yale Child Study Center Partnership: Offering Hope for Abused Children*. N.p.: Safe Horizons and the Yale Child Study Center. https://docplayer.net/48394681-Safe-horizon-yale-child-study-center.html.

McCabe, K. M., M. Yeh, A. F. Garland, and A. Lau. 2005. "The GANA Program: A Tailoring Approach to Adapting Parent Child Interaction Therapy for Mexican Americans." *Education & Treatment of Children* 28, no. 2: 111–129.

McIntosh, P. 1989. "White Privilege: Unpacking the Invisible Knapsack." *Peace and Freedom* (July/August): 10–12.

Mehta, S. 2015. "There's Only One Country That Hasn't Ratified the Convention on Children's Rights: US." American Civil Liberties Union. https://www.aclu.org/blog/human-rights/treaty-ratification/theres-only-one-country-hasnt-ratified-convention-childrens.

Miles, J. R., C. Anders, D. M. Kivlighan III, and A. A. Belcher Platt. 2021. "Cultural Ruptures: Addressing Microaggressions in Group Therapy." *Group Dynamics: Theory, Research, and Practice* 25, no. 1: 74–88.

Miller, J. B., and I. P. Stiver. 1997. *The Healing Connection; How Women Form Relationships in Therapy And in Life*. Beacon Press.

Miller, O., and A. Esenstad. 2015. "Strategies to Reduce Racially Di Spinazzola rate Outcomes in Child Welfare: A National Scan." N.p.: Center for the Study of Social Policy, Alliance for Racial Equity in Child Welfare.

Miller, W. R, and S. Rollnick. 2012. *Motivational interviewing: Helping people change*. 3rd edition. New York: Guilford Press.

Milne, B. 2013. *The History and Theory of Children's Citizenship in Contemporary Societies*. N.p.: SpringerLink.

Moane, G. 2003. "Bridging the Personal and the Political: Practices for a Liberation Psychology." *American Journal of Community Psychology* 31, no. 1–2: 91–101.

Molnar, B. E., and M. R. Beardslee. 2014. "Community-Level Prevention of Child Maltreatment." In *Child Maltreatment: Contemporary Issues in Research and Policy*, Vol 2, edited by J. E. Korbin and R. D. Krugman, 301–316. New York: Springer.

Namy, S., C. Carlson, K. O'Hara, J. Nakuti, P. Bukuluki, J. Lwanyaaga, et al. 2017. "Towards a Feminist Understanding of Intersecting Violence against Women and Children in the Family." *Social Science & Medicine* 184: 40–48.

Napikoski, L. 2020. "Womanist: Definition and Examples—Alice Walker's Term for Black Feminism." ThoughtCo. September 11. https://www.thoughtco.com/womanist-feminism-definition-3528993.

National Association of Social Workers (NASW). 2013. *NASW Standards for Social Work Practice in Child Welfare.* https://www.socialworkers.org/LinkClick.aspx?fileticket=zV1G_96nWoI%3d&portalid=0.

———. (2017) 2021. *Code of Ethics.* Accessed January 7, 2022. https://www.socialworkers.org/About/Ethics/Code-of-Ethics.

National Center for Education Statistics. 2017. *Student Readiness and Progress through School.* https://nces.ed.gov/programs/statereform.

National Child Traumatic Stress Network (NCTSN) 2008. *Culture-Specific Information: Parent-Child Interaction Therapy (PCIT).* https://www.nctsn.org/sites/default/files/interventions/pcit_culture_specific_fact_sheet.pdf.

———. 2012. Trauma-Focused Cognitive Behavioral Therapy. https://www.nctsn.org/interventions/trauma-focused-cognitive-behavioral-therapy.

———. 2019. PCIT: Parent-Child Interaction Therapy. https://www.nctsn.org/sites/default/files/interventions/pcit_general_031419.pdf.

———. N.d. Healthcare. Accessed January 7, 2022. https://www.nctsn.org/trauma-informed-care/creating-trauma-informed-systems/healthcare.

National Scientific Council on the Developing Child. 2020. *Connecting the Brain to the Rest of the Body: Early Childhood Development and Lifelong Health Are Deeply Intertwined.* Working Paper 15. Cambridge, MA: Center on the Developing Child at Harvard University, www.developingchild.harvard.edu.

National Sexual Violence Resource Center. 2015. *Statistics About Sexual Violence.* https://www.nsvrc.org/sites/default/files/publications_nsvrc_factsheet_media-packet_statistics-about-sexual-violence_0.pdf.

National Women's Law Center. N.d. Data on Poverty and Income. Accessed January 10, 2022. https://nwlc.org/issue/data-on-poverty-income/.

Nelson, G., M. Laurendeau, and C. Chamberland. 2001. "Review of Programs to Promote Family Wellness and Prevent the Maltreatment of Children. *Canadian Journal of Behavioural Science* 33, no. 1: 1–13.

Neville, H. A., and G. H. Awad. 2014. "Why Racial Color-Blindness Is Myopic." *American Psychologist* 69, no. 3: 313–314.

New Jersey Department of Children and Families. N.d. Institutional Abuse Investigation Unit. Accessed January 10, 2022. https://www.nj.gov/dcf/about/divisions/iaiu/.

Oberg, C., C. Kivlahan, R. Mishori, W. Martinez, J. R. Gutierrez, Z. Noor, and J. Goldhagen. 2021. "Treatment of Migrant Children on the US Southern Border Is Consistent with Torture." *Pediatrics* 147, no. 1: 1–3.

O'Neill, K.M.G., F. Cluxton-Keller, L. Burrell, S. S. Crowne, and A. Duggan. 2020. "Impact of a Child Abuse Primary Prevention Strategy for New Mothers." *Prevention Science* 21: 4–14.

O'Reilly, M. 2020. "Systems Centered Language: Speaking Truth to Power During COVID-19 while Confronting Racism." Meag-gan O'Reilly,

Ph.D., June 5. https://medium.com/@meagoreillyphd/systems-centered
-language-a3dc7951570e.

Osofsky, J. D. 2003. "Prevalence of Children's Exposure to Domestic
Violence and Child Maltreatment: Implications for Prevention and
Intervention." *Child Clinical and Family Psychology Review* 6, no. 3:
161–170.

Oyserman, D., and S.W.S. Lee. 2008. "Does Culture Influence What and
How We Think? Effects of Priming Individualism and Collectivism."
Psychological Bulletin 134, no. 2: 311–342.

Paez, M., L. R. and Albert. 2012. "Cultural Consciousness." In *Encyclopedia
of Diversity in Education*, edited by J. A. Banks. Thousand Oaks, CA:
Sage Publications.

Pedersen, P. 1990. "The Multicultural Perspective as a Fourth Force in
Counseling." *Journal of Mental Health Counseling* 12, no. 1: 93–95.

Pelton, L. H. 2015. "The Continuing Role of Material Factors in Child
Maltreatment and Placement." *Child Abuse and Neglect* 41: 30–39.

Peterson, P. E. 1993. "Give Kids the Vote." *Harper's Magazine* 286, no. 23
(Feb. 1).

Phillimore, S. 2018. "Mothers Are More Likely to Abuse Children. Fact?"
Child Protection Resource, June 6. http://childprotectionresource
.online/mothers-are-more-likely-to-abuse-children-than-fathers-fact/.

Raman, S., and D. Hodes. 2012. "Cultural Issues in Child Maltreatment."
Journal of Paediatrics and Child Health 48, no. 1: 30–37.

Renzaho A.M.N., and S. Vignjevic. 2011. "The Impact of a Parenting
Intervention in Australia among Migrants and Refugees from Liberia,
Sierra Leone, Congo, and Burundi: Results from the African Migrant
Parenting Program." *Journal of Family Studies* 17, no. 1: 71–79.

Rodriguez, G. 2014. "How Diversity Makes Us Smarter." *Time*. https://time
.com/2973809/immigration-diversity-smarter/.

Saleem, F. T., and S. F. Lambert. 2016. "Differential Effects of Racial
Socialization Messages for African American Adolescents: Personal
Versus Institutional Racial Discrimination." *Journal of Child and Family
Studies* 25, no. 5: 1385–1396.

Salter, P., and G. Adams. 2013. "Toward Critical Race Psychology." *Social
and Personality Compass* 7, no. 11: 781–793.

Sandstrom, A. 2016. "Most States Allow Religious Exemptions from Child
Abuse and Neglect Laws." Pew Research Center, August 12. https://
www.pewresearch.org/fact-tank/2016/08/12/most-states-allow-religious
-exemptions-from-child-abuse-and-neglect-laws/.

Schwartz, S. J., J. B. Unger, B. L. Zamboanga, and J. Szapocznik. 2010.
"Rethinking the Concept of Acculturation: Implications for Theory And
Research." *American Psychologist* 65, no. 4, 237–251.

Sexton, T., and C. W. Turner. 2010. "The Effectiveness of Functional Family
Therapy (FFT) for Youth with Behavioral Problems in a Community
Practice Setting." *Journal of Family Psychology* 24, no. 3: 339–348.

Shin, R. Q. 2015. "The Application of Critical Consciousness and Intersectionality as Tools for De-Colonizing Racial/Ethnic Identity Development Models in the Fields of Counseling and Psychology." In *Decolonizing "Multicultural" Counseling and Psychology: Visions for Social Justice Theory and Practice*, edited by R. Goodman and P. Gorski, 11–22. New York: Springer.

Silva, J. 2011. *ACT Facilitator Manual: Raising Safe Kids Program*. Washington, DC: American Psychological Association.

Singer, R., and M. Fuentes. 2018. "Ethical Issues Associated with Mental Health Interventions for Immigrants and Refugees." In *The Cambridge Handbook of Applied Psychological Ethics*, edited by M. Leach and E. Welfel, 384–405. Cambridge Handbooks in Psychology. Cambridge, UK: Cambridge University Press. https://doi.org/10.1017/9781316417287.020.

Singer, R. R., and P. Tummala-Narra. 2013. "White Clinicians' Perspectives on Working with Racial Minority Immigrant Clients." *Professional Psychology: Research and Practice* 44, no. 5: 290–298.

Speakman, K. 2021. "These States Have Banned Schools from Requiring Covid Vaccination and Masks." *Forbes*, July 16. https://www.forbes.com/sites/kimberleespeakman/2021/07/16/these-states-have-banned-schools-from-requiring-covid-vaccination-and-masks/.

Spinazzola, J., H. Hodgdon, L. Liang, J. D. Ford, C. M. Layne, R. Pynoos, E. C. Briggs, B. Stolbach, and C. Kisiel. 2014. "Unseen Wounds: The Contribution of Psychological Maltreatment to Child and Adolescent Mental Health and Risk Outcomes." *Psychological Trauma: Theory, Research, Practice, and Policy* 6, no. S1: S18–S28.

Staats, C. 2015. *State of the Science: Implicit Bias Review 2014*. Columbus, OH: Kirwan Institute for the Study of Race and Ethnicity. http://kirwaninstitute.osu.edu/wp-content/uploads/2014/03/2014-implicit-bias.pdf.

Stark, E., and A. H. Flitcraft. 1988. Women and Children at Risk: A Feminist Perspective on Child Abuse. *International Journal of Health Services* 18, no. 1: 97–118.

Steele, C. M. 2011. *Whistling Vivaldi: How Stereotypes Affect Us and What We Can Do*. New York: W. W. Norton & Company, Inc.

Sue, D. W., C. M. Capodilupo, G. C. Torino, J. M. Bucceri, A.M.B. Holder, K. L. Nadal, and M. Esquilin. 2007. "Racial Microaggressions in Everyday Life: Implications for Clinical Practice." *American Psychologist* 62, no. 4: 271–286.

Sue, D. W., and D. Sue, D. 2012. *Counseling the Culturally Different: Theory and Practice*. 6th edition. Hoboken, NJ: John Wiley & Sons, Inc.

———. 2016. *Counseling the Culturally Diverse: Theory and Practice*. 7th edition. Hoboken, NJ: John Wiley & Sons, Inc.

Sue, D. W., C. Z. Calle, N. Mendez, S. Alsaidi, and E. Glaeser. 2021. *Microintervention Strategies: What You Can Do to Disarm and*

Dismantle Individual and Systemic Racism and Bias. Hoboken, NJ: John Wiley & Sons, Inc.

Szto, M. 2013. "Real Estate Agents as Agents of Social Change: Redlining, Reverse Redlining, and Greenlining." *Seattle Journal for Social Justice* 12: 1–59.

Thoma, B. C., T. L. Rezeppa, S. Choukas-Bradley, R. H. Salk, and M. P. Marshal. 2021. "Disparities in Childhood Abuse Between Transgender and Cisgender Adolescents." *Pediatrics* 148, no.2: e2020016907. https://doi.org/10.1542/peds.2020-016907.

Tjaden, P., and N. Thoennes. 2000. "Full Report of the Prevalence, Incidence, and Consequences of Violence against Women." Washington, DC: U.S. Department of Justice. https://www.ncjrs.gov/pdffiles1/nij /183781.pdf.

Trickett, P., K. K. Kim, and J. Prindle. 2011. "Variations in Emotional Abuse Experiences Among Multiply Maltreated Young Adolescents and Relations with Developmental Outcomes." *Child Abuse & Neglect* 35, no. 10: 876–886.

Trimble, J. E., and R. Dickson. 2005. "Ethnic Gloss." In *Encyclopedia of Applied Developmental Science,* Vol. 1, edited by C. B. Fisher and R. M. Lerner, 412–415. Thousand Oaks, CA: Sage Publications.

Turner, C. W., M. S. Robbins, S. Rowlands, L. R. and Weaver. 2017. "Summary of Comparison between FFT-CW and Usual Care Sample from Administration and Children's Services." *Child Abuse and Neglect* 69: 85–95.

UNICEF. 2018. *Comprehensive Laws and Social Changes Are Key to Eradicate the Physical Punishment Suffered by 1 Out of Every 2 Children in Latin America and the Caribbean.* Press release, April 25. https://www .unicef.org/lac/en/press-releases/comprehensive-laws-and-social-changes -are-key-eradicate-physical-punishment-suffered.

———. N.d.-a. What Are Human Rights? Accessed January 10, 2022. https://www.unicef.org/child-rights-convention/what-are-human-rights.

———. N.d.-b. What Is the Convention on the Rights of the Child? Accessed January 10, 2022. https://www.unicef.org/child-rights-convention/what-is -the-convention.

———. N.d.-c. History of Child Rights. Accessed January 10, 2022. https://www.unicef.org/child-rights-convention/history-child-rights.

U.S. Department of Health & Human Services (HHS), Administration for Children and Families, Administration on Children, Youth and Families (ACYF), and the Children's Bureau. (2018). *Child Maltreatment 2016.* https://www.acf.hhs.gov/sites/default/files/documents/cb /cm2016.pdf.

———. (2021). *Child Maltreatment 2019.* https://www.acf.hhs.gov/sites /default/files/documents/cb/cm2019.pdf.

U.S. Department of Justice. 2011. *Characteristics of Suspected Human Trafficking Incidents, 2008–2010.* April. https://bjs.ojp.gov/content/pub /pdf/cshti0810.pdf.

Van Mourik, K., M. R. Crone, M. S. de Wolff, and R. Reis. 2017. "Parent Training Programs for Ethnic Minorities: A Meta-Analysis of Adaptations and Effect." *Prevention Science* 18, no. 1: 95–105.

Vial, A., C. van der Put, G.J.J.M. Stams, K. Kossakowski, and M. Assink. 2020. "Exploring the Interrelatedness of Risk Factors for Child Maltreatment: A Network Approach." *Child Abuse and Neglect* 107 (Sept.).

Vontress, C. E. 1971. Racial Differences: Impediments to Rapport. *Journal of Counseling Psychology* 18, no. 1: 7–13.

Walker, N. E., C. M. Brooks, and L. S. Wrightsman. 1999. *Children's Rights in the United States: In Search of a National Policy.* Thousand Oaks, CA: Sage Publications.

Wray-Lake, L., R. Wells, L. Alvis, S. Delgado, A. K. Syvertsen, and A. Metzger. 2018. "Being a Latinx Adolescent Under a Trump Presidency: Analysis of Latinx Youth's Reactions to Immigration Politics." *Children and Youth Services Review* 87: 192–204.

White-Johnson, R. L., K. R. Ford, and R. M. Sellers. 2010. "Parental Racial Socialization Profiles: Association with Demographic Factors, Racial Discrimination, Childhood Socialization, and Racial Identity." *Cultural Diversity and Ethnic Minority Psychology* 16, no. 2: 237–247.

Widom, C. S. 2014. "Longterm Consequences of Child Maltreatment." In *Handbook of Child Maltreatment*, edited by J. E. Korbin and R. D. Krugman, 225–247. New York: Springer.

Williams, J. H., R. A. Van Dorn, C. L. Bright, M. Jonson-Reid, and V. E. Nebbitt. 2010. "Child Maltreatment and Delinquency Onset among African American Adolescent Males." *Research on Social Work Practice* 20, no. 3: 253–259.

Wolff, J., and D. Leopold. 2021. "Karl Marx," *The Stanford Encyclopedia of Philosophy* (Spring 2021 Edition), edited by E. N. Zalta. https://plato .stanford.edu/archives/spr2021/entries/marx/.

World Health Organization (WHO). 2020. *Addressing Violence against Children, Women and Older People during the COVID-19 Pandemic: Key Actions*. https://www.who.int/publications/i/item/WHO-2019-nCoV -Violence_actions-2020.1.

Yoo, H. C., K. S. Burrola, and M. F. Steger. 2010. "A Preliminary Report on a New Measure: Internalization of the Model Minority Myth Measure (IM-4) and Its Psychological Correlates among Asian American College Students." *Journal of Counseling Psychology* 57, no. 1: 114–127.

Index

About the Authors

MILTON A. FUENTES is a professor of psychology at Montclair State University in Montclair, New Jersey, and a licensed psychologist in New Jersey and New York. His scholarship focuses on equity, diversity, and inclusion, and he has authored several peer-reviewed articles, book chapters, and books in this area. Fuentes also coauthored a manual with Julia Silva for facilitators of the ACT Raising Safe Kids Program, an international parenting program housed at the American Psychological Association. In this manual, he applies the principles of motivational interviewing to the program's parenting sessions, promoting child welfare and discouraging child maltreatment.

RACHEL R. SINGER is a clinical director of an outpatient private practice in Rockville, Maryland, providing treatment to clients of all ages. She has co-written book chapters on case conceptualizations of immigrant clients with Milton A. Fuentes and on ethical issues in working with refugees, asylees, and immigrants with Renee L. DeBoard-Lucas.

RENEE L. DEBOARD-LUCAS treats trauma in youth and adults at a private practice in Washington, DC. She is co-founder of The TRUE Center which provides trauma intervention and prevention services, regardless of ability to pay. She has authored publications on child trauma and mental health needs among refugees and immigrants, some with Rachel R. Singer.

THE PREVENTING CHILD MALTREATMENT COLLECTION

PREVENTING CHILD MALTREATMENT IN THE U.S.: MULTICULTURAL CONSIDERATIONS
Milton A. Fuentes, Rachel R. Singer, and Renee L. DeBoard-Lucas
9781978822573 Paper
9781978822580 Cloth

PREVENTING CHILD MALTREATMENT IN THE U.S.: THE LATINX COMMUNITY PERSPECTIVE
Esther J. Calzada, Monica Faulkner, Catherine LaBrenz, and Milton A. Fuentes
9781978822887 Paper
9781978822894 Cloth

PREVENTING CHILD MALTREATMENT IN THE U.S.: AMERICAN INDIAN AND ALASKA NATIVE PERSPECTIVES
Royleen J. Ross, Julii M. Green, and Milton A. Fuentes
9781978821101 Paper
9781978821118 Cloth

PREVENTING CHILD MALTREATMENT IN THE U.S.: THE BLACK COMMUNITY PERSPECTIVE
Melissa Phillips, Shavonne J. Moore-Lobban, and Milton A. Fuentes
9781978820630 Paper
9781978820647 Cloth

The Preventing Child Maltreatment collection is a four-book miniseries within the Violence Against Women and Children series at Rutgers University Press. This collection, curated by Milton A. Fuentes from Montclair State University, is devoted to advancing an understanding of the dynamics of child maltreatment across ethnically diverse populations. Starting with *Preventing Child Maltreatment in the U.S.: Multicultural Considerations*, which provides a general examination of child maltreatment through the interaction of feminist, multicultural, and social justice lenses, the rest of the series takes a closer look at Native American/Alaska Native, Black, and Latinx communities in order to provide insight for social workers who may encounter those populations within their scope of treatment. Policymakers, practitioners, graduate students, and social workers of all kinds will find this collection of great interest.

RRUTGERSUNIVERSITY**PRESS**
rutgersuniversitypress.org

Printed in the United States
by Baker & Taylor Publisher Services